PHPEclipse: A User Guide

Shu-Wai Chow

BIRMINGHAM - MUMBAI

PHPEclipse: A User Guide

First published: January 2006

Published by Packt Publishing Ltd.
32 Lincoln Road
Olton
Birmingham, B27 6PA, UK.

ISBN 1-904811-44-2

www.packtpub.com

Cover Design by www.visionwt.com

Credits

Author
Shu-Wai Chow

Reviewer
Thomas M. Ose

Technical Editor
Nikhil Bangera

Editorial Manager
Dipali Chittar

Development Editor
Douglas Paterson

Indexer
Ashutosh Pande

Proofreader
Chris Smith

Production Coordinator
Manjiri Nadkarni

Cover Designer
Helen Wood

About the Author

Shu-Wai Chow has worked in the field of computer programming and information technology for the past eight years. He started his career in Sacramento, California, spending four years as the webmaster for Educaid, a First Union company and another four years at Vision Service Plan as an application developer. Through the years, he has become proficient in Java, JSP, PHP, ColdFusion, ASP, LDAP, XSLT, and XSL-FO. Shu has also been the volunteer webmaster and a feline adoption counselor for several animal welfare organizations in Sacramento.

He is currently a software engineer at Antenna Software in Jersey City, New Jersey.

Born in the British Crown Colony of Hong Kong, Shu did most of his alleged growing up in Palo Alto, California. He studied Anthropology and Economics at California State University, Sacramento. He lives along the New Jersey coast with seven very demanding cats, three birds that are too smart for their own good, a cherished Fender Stratocaster, and a beloved, saint-like girlfriend.

Acknowledgements

To Nora Lynn... Your support, love, and wisdom through the years have been invaluable.

First and foremost, I would like to thank the people at Packt Publishing for this opportunity and their confidence. I would especially like to thank my Development Editor, Douglas Paterson, for his support, good humor, and, above all, patience. Also at Packt, I would like to thank Nikhil Bangera for his diligence. Thanks to Thomas Ose, the Reviewer, for his insight.

My gratitude goes to the developers of Eclipse, PHPEclipse, and their respective user communities. Special thanks to Michael Huetteman for all his assistance, and Charles Perkonig and Robert Kraske for their work on the PHPEclipse debugger clients. You have created products that make a lot of people's lives easier. Thanks, also, to John Starkey, of PHPBuilder.com, who gave me a forum to write my first two articles.

Thanks to Patricia Quinn, Stuart Montgomery, and Kari McKinney who did their best to keep me on track through their encouraging words and shameful berating.

Career-wise, I would like to thank Gary Sandler, who gave me my first 'big break' in programming and information technology. A mentor and teacher in every sense of the words, I would not be doing what I'm doing today if it wasn't for him.

I hereby give a stern, solemn nod to Sascha Goldstein and Curtis Portwood.

I would be remiss if I didn't mention all our various animal companions in such an enduring setting, so here goes: (in order of feline hierarchy) Snowball, Lizzie Borden, Saffy, Pim Pim, Tera-San, Mathilda, Manfred, (in order of avian hierarchy) Avi, Hoser, and Dolly. And the ones that are gone but not forgotten: Malachi, Macaroni, Natasha, Squishy, and Marsha.

And last but not least, thanks to Anneliese Strunk. You'll have to wait for the next book to get a dedication, but until then, you have my heart.

About the Reviewer

Thomas M. Ose has been actively involved in computer and information technologies for the past 28 years. He has seen computer and software trends and technology mature over various industries including the manufacturing, office automation, and communication sectors. Over the years Thomas has been a programmer, consultant, and manager for various industries; and he has become proficient in many languages and disciplines, including C, C++, C#, PHP, Java, XML, and UML. He prides himself on always learning something new and developing applications and solutions at the cutting edge of technology and the industry.

Thomas is currently President of his own consulting company, Ose Micro Solutions, Inc. specializing in electronic B2B, G2B system for the Uniform Commercial Code and Business Registration systems at state and local governments. For his solutions, he utilizes PHP, Java, and C# to provide web service- and browser-based solutions using XML to file regulatory documents at state and local governments. He has developed many national standards in this area and has spoken at numerous trade conventions.

Table of Contents

Preface

The PHP language has come a long way from its humble roots as a set of Perl scripts written by Rasmus Lerdorf. Today, PHP enjoys enormous market share and the latest release, PHP 5, sports a robust object-oriented programming model. Naturally, development practices have also matured. Those of us who taught ourselves PHP in the late nineties have become more sophisticated in our coding techniques. PHP has also made significant headway into corporate environments. Both changes have led to a demand for tools that make development easier, faster, and more integrated with other systems such as databases and version-control tools.

Our tool selections, however, have historically been one of two extremes. On one hand are the editors. Fundamentally, these are text editors with basic development tools slapped on. While affordable, they lacked features that made them a true integrated development environment (IDE). To get these features, we had to purchase powerful and expensive IDEs. Even then, our choices were limited to NuSphere's PhpED or Zend Studio.

Things began to change in 2001. IBM released Eclipse, a powerful Java IDE, as an open source project. Developers saw the potential of Eclipse's extensible, plug-in-based architecture. Thanks to this community, Eclipse soon became much more than an editor and spoke many more languages than just Java. In 2003, a team of developers released the PHPEclipse plug-in. Finally the gap between PHP and Eclipse was closed. Developers now have a free and powerful IDE for PHP development.

In this book, we will explore using Eclipse for PHP web development using the PHPEclipse plug-in. We will take a tutorial-style approach throughout most of this book. Installation and setup walkthroughs are provided. Features of Eclipse and PHPEclipse that are helpful for PHP development will be explained.

What This Book Covers

This book is organized to get you quickly up and running with Eclipse for PHP development. The beginning chapters cover the basics of Eclipse, and then we move on to writing PHP code in Eclipse. From there, we move to more advanced features that are helpful, but not essential for PHP development, like source-code control and database querying.

Chapter 1 covers Eclipse's history and its architecture, and introduces PHPEclipse.

In *Chapter 2*, we install the necessary core software for developing applications in PHPEclipse— Apache, PHP, Java, Eclipse, and PHPEclipse.

Chapter 3 explains the feature of the Eclipse interface and how to customize it.

Chapter 4 is where we start writing PHP code. We will go through creating a project and examine in depth the features available in PHPEclipse for PHP development.

In *Chapter 5,* we debug our application. We will explain debugging terms and concepts, and how Eclipse debugs. This chapter covers the installation and setting up of the DBG debugger.

In *Chapter 6*, we set up the Quantum DB plug-in and learn how to use it to manipulate databases. We will also install a JDBC driver and connect to it using the Quantum DB plug-in.

In *Chapter 7*, we explore the CVS integration of Eclipse. We will show how to manage and store a project completely in CVS as well as explain general CVS and versioning concepts.

Finally, in *Chapter 8*, we publish our website to a web server. We will use Eclipse's Update Manager to add an FTP client functionality.

What You Need for This Book

To get all you can out of this book, you should have a computer running Mac OS X, Linux or UNIX with X, or Microsoft Windows 2000 or greater. From a hardware standpoint, Eclipse likes more of everything.

You should also have privileges to install system and server software on the machine. What follows is a list of software we will be installing:

Server Software

- Apache
- PHP
- MySQL (optional)
- JDBC (optional)
- DBG Debugger (optional)
- CVS (optional)

Workstation Software

- Java
- Eclipse
- PHPEclipse

Conventions

In this book, you will find a number of styles of text that distinguish between different kinds of information. Here are some examples of these styles, and an explanation of their meaning.

There are three styles for code. Code words in text are shown as follows: "We can include other contexts through the use of the `include` directive."

A block of code will be set as follows:

```php
public function getACat($id, $dbConn)
  {
    $sql = "SELECT * FROM tCat WHERE CatID = " . $id;
    $e = mysql_query($sql, $dbConn);
    return mysql_fetch_array($e);
  }
```

When we wish to draw your attention to a particular part of a code block, the relevant lines or items will be made bold:

```php
<?php
  include("../classes/clsHeader.php");
  include("../classes/clsDatabase.php");
  $dbConn = new clsDatabase();
?>
```

Any command-line input and output is written as follows:

```
mysql> SELECT * FROM tCat;
```

New terms and **important words** are introduced in a bold-type font. Words that you see on the screen, in menus or dialog boxes for example, appear in our text like this: "clicking the Next button moves you to the next screen".

> Warnings or important notes appear in a box like this.

Tips and tricks appear like this.

Reader Feedback

Feedback from our readers is always welcome. Let us know what you think about this book, what you liked or may have disliked. Reader feedback is important for us to develop titles that you really get the most out of.

To send us general feedback, simply drop an email to feedback@packtpub.com, making sure to mention the book title in the subject of your message.

If there is a book that you need and would like to see us publish, please send us a note in the SUGGEST A TITLE form on www.packtpub.com or email suggest@packtpub.com.

If there is a topic that you have expertise in and you are interested in either writing or contributing to a book, see our author guide on www.packtpub.com/authors.

Customer Support

Now that you are the proud owner of a Packt book, we have a number of things to help you to get the most from your purchase.

Downloading the Example Code for the Book

Visit http://www.packtpub.com/support, and select this book from the list of titles to download any example code or extra resources for this book. The files available for download will then be displayed.

> The downloadable files contain instructions on how to use them.

Errata

Although we have taken every care to ensure the accuracy of our contents, mistakes do happen. If you find a mistake in one of our books—maybe a mistake in text or code—we would be grateful if you would report this to us. By doing this you can save other readers from frustration, and help to improve subsequent versions of this book. If you find any errata, report them by visiting http://www.packtpub.com/support, selecting your book, clicking on the Submit Errata link, and entering the details of your errata. Once your errata have been verified, your submission will be accepted and the errata added to the list of existing errata. The existing errata can be viewed by selecting your title from http://www.packtpub.com/support.

Questions

You can contact us at questions@packtpub.com if you are having a problem with some aspect of the book, and we will do our best to address it.

1

Overview of Eclipse and PHPEclipse

The impact that the Eclipse Platform has made on application development is amazing and unprecedented in many ways. From the story of its birth to its wide feature set, there is nothing bland about this product. The Platform has created commercial product opportunities around it and gives a bountiful amount of freedom and control to end users. This has led to widespread industry adoption and corporate support.

The Platform's best known component, the **Integrated Development Environment (IDE)**, alone is on par with, if not outright excels against, many similar commercial offerings. Originally a Java IDE, Eclipse makes an excellent PHP development environment with the help of the PHPEclipse plug-in. PHP developers experienced with IDEs will enjoy its extensibility and power and if you have never used an IDE on a PHP project, Eclipse is a great tool to get started with. It has everything you would need in an IDE, runs on many platforms, and best of all, it's completely free.

Integrated Development Environments

IDEs are simply programs to write programs. They are generally editing environments with tools to help programmers write code quickly and efficiently. As an example, we can create PHP-driven web applications using a combination of Eclipse and PHPEclipse. Core features typically include:

- **Code completion or code insight**: The ability of an IDE to *know* a language's keywords and function names is crucial. The IDE may use this knowledge to do such things as highlight typographic errors, suggest a list of available functions based on the appropriate situation, or offer a function's definition from the official documentation.

- **Resource management**: When creating applications, languages often rely on certain resources, like library or header files, to be at specific locations. IDEs should be able to manage these resources. An IDE should be aware of any required resources so that errors can be spotted at the development stage and not later, in the compile or build stage.

- **Debugging tools**: In an IDE, you should be able to thoroughly test your application before release. The IDE may be able to give variable values at certain points, connect to different data repositories, or accept different run-time parameters.

- **Compile and build**: For languages that require a compile or build stage, IDEs translate code from high-level languages to the object code of the targeted platform.

Requirements for these features vary substantially from language to language. Thus, traditionally, an IDE specializes in one language or a set of similar languages. Some famous IDEs and their languages include: JBuilder for Java; Metrowerks CodeWarrior suite for Java, C, and C++; and Microsoft's Visual Studio for its Visual Basic and C# family of languages.

Advantages of Using an IDE

Using an IDE will save you a lot of effort in writing a program. Some advantages include:

1. **Less time and effort**: The entire purpose of an IDE is to make developing faster and easier. Its tools and features are supposed to help you organize resources, prevent mistakes, and provide shortcuts.

2. **Enforce project or company standards**: Simply by working in the same development environment, a group of programmers will adhere to a standard way of doing things. Standards can be further enforced if the IDE offers predefined templates, or if code libraries are shared between different team members/teams working on the same project.

3. **Project management**: This can be twofold. First, many IDEs have documentation tools that either automate the entry of developer comments, or may actually force developers to write comments in different areas. Second, simply by having a visual presentation of resources, it should be a lot easier to know how an application is laid out as opposed to traversing the file system for arcane files in the file system.

Disadvantages of Using an IDE

Be careful of some of the pitfalls of using an IDE as it may not be ideal for everyone and might not be suitable in every situation.

1. **Learning curve**: IDEs are complicated tools. Maximizing their benefit will require time and patience.

2. **A sophisticated IDE may not be a good tool for beginning programmers**: If you throw the learning curve of an IDE on top of learning how to program, it can be quite frustrating. Further, features and shortcuts for experienced programmers often hide crucial but mundane details of a language. Details should not be overlooked when learning a new language. Using an IDE may hamper the learning of a new language.

3. **Will not fix bad code, practices, or design**: You still need to be proficient and meticulous. An IDE will not eliminate efficiency or performance problems in your application. IDEs are like paintbrushes. Whether you create a Van Gogh or a Velvet Elvis is dictated by your skill and decisions.

IDEs in Development Projects

There are many ways to create an application. Plenty of pundits and consultants have become wealthy by creating and pitching system development lifecycle models to companies. Not surprisingly, having many ways of doing something leads to many diverse development models. In each model, steps may be called different things, will have different collaborators, and may even occur in different orders. However, most have these steps in common:

- **Requirements Gathering**: What do you want the program to do?
- **System Design**: How is the program designed? What is the structure of the program? How does it interact with other systems? How will the program address each identified requirement?
- **Development**: Code is written at this stage.
- **Testing**: Does the application work? Will the program negatively affect other existing systems?
- **Acceptance**: Do your customers actually like the product? Will it fulfill their business needs?
- **Deployment**: Pushing the code out to production.

It is not uncommon for each step to use different tools. You may simply use a word processor for the requirements gathering. If you use **Unified Modeling Language** (UML) for system design, you'll need a graphical diagramming tool. Traditional IDEs are used in the development stage to write code. An IDE may have a debugger to help with testing, or deployment tools, but this is not always the case. If you use a simple editor like Macromedia HomeSite, you'll certainly need other tools to test and deploy, and even build if necessary.

An IDE, therefore, is just one tool used in developing an application. As one would expect, use of multiple tools drives up development costs by way of license purchases, training, and integration hassles. Eclipse, however, was built to solve this problem.

Eclipse

A very simplified definition of Eclipse is that it's an IDE. Out of the box, it is an excellent Java IDE. However, it goes beyond that. Eclipse is based on modules, called plug-ins, which can extend it beyond just writing code. The number of plug-ins available in the Eclipse community is enormous and they cover diverse functionalities. Using plug-ins, we can write programs in any language, including PHP. We can also use plug-ins to perform any task in our development process, from the idea stage of drawing diagrams to the development stage of writing code to the deployment stage of pushing files to a production server.

A History of Eclipse

For most software applications, we wouldn't need to care about their history or who develops them. Most IDEs are developed by a commercial company and sold for profit to other developers. For those IDEs, previous versions or incarnations only matter to determine upgrade prices.

However, Eclipse is not your typical software application. It's not only interesting to know its pedigree, but it's important as well. Knowing its history and who exactly drives development will help you appreciate Eclipse's architecture, understand some quirks you may encounter, guide you to the proper place to ask for help, and perhaps inspire you to participate in the community of Eclipse developers.

IBM and OTI

Before Java, the object oriented language that was all the rage was Smalltalk. **Object Technologies International (OTI)** specialized in development tools for Smalltalk. Among these tools was Envy, a development environment and source-code manager. In 1996, IBM purchased OTI and made it a subsidiary company. Using Envy as a model, the two companies collaborated to create next generation development tools for languages like Smalltalk (Visual Age for Smalltalk) and Java (Visual Age for Java).

Their next collaboration on development tools began in 1999. Development would occur against the backdrop of two industry trends. First, Linux and open source were emerging as major forces in the industry. Seizing on this, IBM developed a 'Linux strategy' and publicly committed $1 billion to marketing Linux and supporting open-source software. Second, in web development, it was clear that typical enterprise web applications often required components to be written in different languages. C++ may be required to access an older data store, SQL may be required to access a more modern database, and JSP may be required to deliver the HTML and JavaScript output. Developers often had to use different programs to write these different portions. IBM wanted to create one unified tool for developers' needs.

In 2001, after a reported development cost of $40 million, the Eclipse Platform was born, which addressed both these industry trends. IBM reaffirmed its Linux strategy by releasing Eclipse as open-source software to the world, and everyone saw how its architecture allowed unparalleled extensibility.

The Eclipse Foundation

IBM did not release Eclipse into the cold, harsh world to fend for itself. It created and funded the **Eclipse Foundation** to act as the custodian of the Eclipse Platform. The Foundation's **Board of Stewards** was to steer the direction of Eclipse, oversee development progress, and evangelize the product. Originally, the consortium comprised representatives from Borland, IBM, Merant, Red Hat, SuSE, Rational Software, QNX, TogetherSoft, and Webgain. Over time, other companies such as Oracle, SAP, Ericsson, Hitachi, Fujitsu, and Intel were granted membership.

In February 2004, IBM officially spun off the Foundation and reorganized it as an independent, not-for-profit corporation. The reasoning was that no one company, not even IBM in this case, could meet all the demands of the customers and by setting the Foundation free, Eclipse could become an even better platform for creating integrated tools. This is being achieved today. More contributors have joined in to help with the development of Eclipse, and its independence gives the Foundation more flexibility in collaborating with other companies.

The Foundation currently manages several Eclipse-related open-source projects. These top-level projects range from business intelligence tools to testing tools and web tools. Underneath each top-level project are smaller subprojects to break down the work.

Originally, there was only one top-level project, the Eclipse project, and its purpose was to manage the IDE that is the subject of this book. That is still the official name for the project despite the use of the word 'Eclipse' to mean more of the Foundation, or the platform depending on the context, rather than the IDE product. A counterpart to this is the Apache Foundation. Originally, Apache just meant a web server, but today, the Apache Foundation hosts many more projects in addition to its flagship, the web server. Unlike Eclipse, though, the Apache Foundation has re-branded the server to 'Apache HTTP Server'. Thus, barring any similar renaming of the Eclipse IDE, the term 'Eclipse project' should be referring to the project in charge of the IDE development and not to the Foundation as a whole or any of the other top-level projects managed by the Foundation. For simplicity sake, though, unless otherwise stated, when we say 'Eclipse' in this book, we'll mean the Eclipse IDE.

The Eclipse project is divided into three subprojects—the **Platform**, **Java Development Tools (JDT)**, and the **Plug-in Development Environment (PDE)**. These three compose the Eclipse **Software Development Kit (SDK)**. The Platform subproject manages the IDE infrastructure and essential services. In other words, the Platform makes the IDE what it is. There are about fifteen smaller component projects underneath the Platform. They include things like **Ant** integration, the core libraries, the text editor, and the help system. The JDT subproject is in charge of the plug-ins that makes Eclipse a world-class Java IDE—right out of the box. Three components compose this subproject—the core Java editing environment, debugger, and user interface (UI). The PDE subproject manages the interface that gives Eclipse its incredible extensibility. **PDE Build** and user interface are the components. As we will soon see, plug-ins are essential to the functionality of Eclipse. The PDE subproject makes interfacing, and thus extending, Eclipse easy. The figure below shows the top-level projects undertaken by the Eclipse Foundation and gives an idea of the sub-projects under the Eclipse Project.

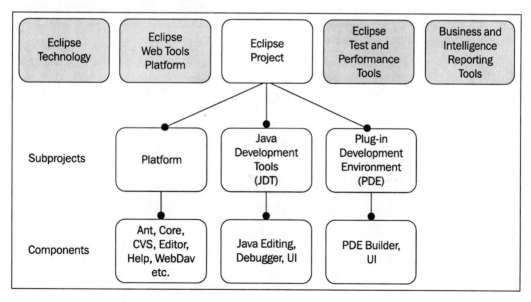

A **Project Management Committee (PMC)** manages the vision and development of the Eclipse project. The PMC Leader, who is appointed by the Board of Directors, generally selects the PMC. Developers are the volunteers who actually write the Eclipse code.

The Eclipse Architecture

Up to this point, we've hinted at how the Eclipse IDE can be your one tool for the whole development process. This seems quite a bold claim, but it is very much a reality with Eclipse thanks to its forward-thinking architecture.

Plug-Ins

By itself, the Eclipse Platform does nothing. The core piece of Eclipse is just a small kernel called the **Platform Runtime**. All functionality of the IDE is a result of interactions between the plug-ins and the kernel. When you launch the Eclipse executable, the kernel checks what plug-ins are available in a special plug-ins directory. Each plug-in has a **manifest file** that defines how it interacts with the Platform and with other plug-ins. To save startup time and system resources, each plug-in is loaded only when necessary.

The manifest file is XML based and defines the extension points used by the plug-in. Extension points are the basis in communications between plug-ins and the Platform. An extension point either declares the services this plug-in can provide to other plug-ins, or declares how this plug-in will interact with another plug-in's extension point. This leads to a very interesting behavior of Eclipse. With plug-ins themselves being extensible, the lines often blur between plug-ins. When we actually start coding in PHP, we'll see how tools in the JDT are extended via the PHPEclipse plug-in. For example, the same tool that is used to show an outline of all functions in a Java class is also used to show PHP functions once PHPEclipse is installed.

When you download the full Eclipse SDK, it includes several plug-ins that give it all the features of an IDE—**workspace**, **Workbench**, the JDT, **Version and Configuration Management (VCM)** system, the help system, and the PDE.

Each application you develop in Eclipse is organized as a project. Each project may hold different files, directories, and settings. The workspace not only manages where the resources are, but also manages the state of resources. Each resource may hold a historical record of changes and other resources might be interested in this information. The workspace coordinates all of these things between resources.

The Workbench is essentially Eclipse's GUI. From menu items to window panes to buttons, the Workbench handles everything you see and interact with. The Workbench is written in the Eclipse **Standard Widget Toolkit (SWT)** and **JFace**. We'll discuss the SWT and JFace in depth later. Basically, like Java's native Swing, both are Java GUI libraries. Like the Workbench and everything else, SWT and JFace are plug-ins that are loaded by the runtime kernel.

Since Eclipse made its name as a Java development platform, the JDT (a Java development plug-in) is included with the standard Eclipse SDK download package. Eclipse's knowledge of Java syntax, compiling, and debugging come from the JDT. A lot of people do not need Eclipse to do anything more than to be a Java IDE. The JDT is what makes Eclipse a Java IDE.

Version and configuration management system, or more commonly referred to as the **Team Tools**, manages source code shared by a team. Essentially, the Team Tools allow Eclipse to act as a full **Concurrent Versioning System (CVS)** client. By talking to the Workbench plug-in, the Team Tools know what files need to be committed and where to place updated files. Branches, tagging, and patches are also managed by the Team Tools. Do not worry if none of this makes sense. We'll explore more about versioning and CVS in Chapter 7.

The help system makes it easy for plug-in developers to create help files and documentation for end users. All the developer needs to do is create the help files in HTML and define the schema using XML. Through the help system, Eclipse pulls in the help file appropriate to the plug-in when requested by the end user.

Finally, in a seemingly circular relationship, the PDE, the tool to create plug-ins, is itself a plug-in. Development and deployment of plug-ins require meticulous attention to detail. The manifest and source code files can grow quite large. The PDE automates much of this work through **wizards**, templates, and Eclipse's own workspace. Thanks to the PDE, it is no surprise that there is a large community of Eclipse plug-ins and plug-in developers. Having a native tool builder within the tool lets anyone alter Eclipse to their own individual liking.

Eclipse plug-in development is a very rich subject. Entire books have been devoted solely to this topic. Be aware that Eclipse plug-ins are written solely in Java using SWT and JFace.

For PHP development, we will be using the PHPEclipse plug-in. This third-party plug-in fits nicely into the Eclipse architecture as can be seen in the figure below which shows the Eclipse Platform architecture:

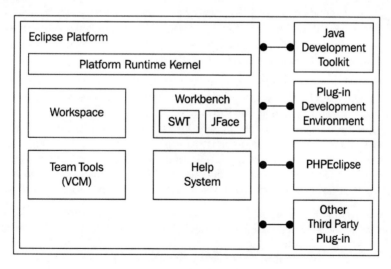

The Workbench Plug-In

Now that we know the roles and workings of plug-ins, the Workbench plug-in deserves a little bit of extra attention. The JDT and PDE plug-ins rely on the Workbench's extension points, but not vice versa. If you do not require Java development tools, you can conceivably download just the Eclipse Platform. The Eclipse home site (`http://eclipse.org/downloads/`) offers downloads of the Platform without the JDT and PDE plug-ins.

The text editor functionality is in the Workbench. These 'platform-only' downloads would have the editor without any sort of indication that this is a Java IDE. The three other 'core' plug-ins (help, workspace, and Team Tools) would also be present. However, Eclipse's functionality would certainly be limited.

The primary purpose of having downloads without the JDT and PDE plug-ins is to allow redistribution and repackaging of Eclipse. If your product involves Eclipse but not Java, you can release a version without the JDT. Another purpose may be to speed up the start-up time and performance of Eclipse. Indeed, the smaller the number of plug-ins that are installed, the faster Eclipse starts up.

Standard Widget Toolkit

The story of the SWT is certainly the most controversial part of the development of Eclipse. SWT does the actual illustration of the Eclipse GUI. Buttons, checkboxes, windows, and the like are all handled by the SWT. If you want to draw a radio button inside a box in a plug-in, you use SWT's API to do so. In fact, we can use SWT as the basis of the GUI for any Java desktop application.

On the other hand, we have Swing. Swing is the official collection of Java classes used to build user interfaces, objects like windows, text boxes, and such. Swing and SWT sound a lot alike. In fact, you might say it sounds like SWT replaces Swing in Eclipse, and you'd be right. In developing Eclipse, IBM bypassed the officially blessed GUI toolkit and created its own. Needless to say, Sun is not very happy with this, and this is perhaps a reason why Sun, the creator of Java, does not hold, and has never held, any role in the Eclipse Foundation.

SWT integrates much closer to the native operating platform than Swing. For each platform that SWT runs on, the libraries hold a direct mapping from the SWT Java calls to the target platform, which are written in C. Unlike Swing, the JVM does not have to do this mapping. This gives SWT applications a speed advantage when dealing with GUIs. The performance of SWT applications is close to OS-native applications. For common widgets like radio buttons and text boxes, SWT uses the operating system's native widgets. Only if a widget is not defined will SWT emulate the widget. An SWT-based application running on Windows XP will look like a Windows XP program. The same program will look like a Mac OS X program when running in Mac OS X.

There are downsides to SWT. First and foremost, by integrating tightly with platforms, the interface loses its consistency, and Java applications potentially lose their portability. Each platform requires its own SWT library, and platform-specific code can be written in each one. This opens the door to platform-specific Java, which is philosophically against Sun's promise of keeping Java platform independent. Since it's not an officially blessed specification, SWT applications are breaking a standard. If you decide take a side in this issue, be aware that you're entering a furious religious debate.

There are technical downsides to SWT too. Since SWT interaction does not happen in the JVM, developers cannot rely on Java's garbage collector to destroy objects. You'll have to be vigilant and do this yourself. Swing also employs a pluggable architecture, which you will lose with SWT.

IBM was well aware of the tradeoffs when creating SWT. In the end, we can't argue with the results. If you have ever used a Swing-based desktop application, you would never guess Eclipse was written in Java. Eclipse is a fast and cross-platform application that aesthetically looks good. Pre-compiled binaries are available for all major operating systems including Mac OS X, Linux (GTK and Motif), Windows, and Solaris. SWT makes Eclipse fast and cross platform.

Why Use Eclipse?

We now have an understanding of Eclipse's history, the components involved, and what makes Eclipse tick. Why should we use Eclipse, especially for PHP development? Why not use one of the traditional PHP IDEs, or why even use an IDE at all? There are plenty of advantages, but the four with the largest impact are the plug-in architecture, its generous license, intellectual freedom, and powerful features.

Eclipse is Extensible

We have explored Eclipse's plug-in architecture from a high-level technical view. Indeed, the technical flexibility is quite impressive. The architecture's impact on the industry and our work processes cannot be overstated. It is the use of plug-ins that enables Eclipse to be the only program you need for all the stages of the application development lifecycle.

Imagine that you are building a new web application written in PHP. You first need to draw UML class, sequence, and activity diagrams. PHP coding will obviously be your principal duty. During development, you realize that you need to update a module written in Python. You may also need to explore a database schema. An LDAP server with group and role definitions will handle security, so you'll need a tool to browse LDAP's schema. As you work, you debug portions of your application and share your changes with other developers on the team. You move the application to one server for the testing team, another server for the acceptance testing team, and finally a production server when you're ready to implement your new application.

All of these tasks can be accomplished directly within Eclipse via external plug-ins. Even better, you do not have to create these plug-ins. A large developer community exists that has created plug-ins to extend Eclipse. Some plug-ins are commercial and require a license; however, many are free and open source. When people say that Eclipse 'enjoys widespread industry support', it is often a reference to the commercial member companies of the Eclipse Foundation. However, it is also an allusion to the many grassroots volunteers and commercial developers who have given Eclipse more functionality by creating new plug-ins.

> Eclipse.org maintains a list of plug-ins, commercial and open source, located at
> http://www.eclipse.org/community. There is also a section with links to plug-in
> community sites that maintain even larger or more specialized lists. In Appendix A,
> we highlight some plug-ins that may be helpful to you in PHP development.

By having all of your tools in Eclipse, you simplify your development environment. Learning curves and software compatibility issues are decreased. Further, since many of the plug-ins are open source, your costs for tools can be lowered.

Eclipse is Free

Eclipse is released under the terms of the **Eclipse Public License** (**EPL**). That is, Eclipse is free and open source. To alleviate any prejudgments and confusion, we need to define what 'free' means, clarify exactly what 'open source' means, and what rights you have under the EPL.

For all practical purposes, 'free' means that Eclipse will not cost you any money to use. There is nothing that you have to pay for—either when you initially obtain the program or by means of upgrade fees or royalties. Someone may sell you Eclipse on a CD, but you do not have to buy it as the same can be legally downloaded from its website.

'Free' also gives you the freedom to redistribute and alter the program as you see fit. For the latter, this also implies that you have the right to access the source code. By definition, freedom does not require you to obtain permission from the original author to redistribute or modify.

'Open source' is a little more complex. Open-source licenses must grant users the basic freedoms explained above. However, they have subtle differences, which lead to larger impacts. One notable and well-publicized difference is whether a license is 'viral' in nature. That is, if you modify a program with your own closed-source proprietary code, your code will fall under the open-source license and you lose all intellectual property rights to it. The most famous viral license is the **GNU Public License** (**GPL**). This has led to unfair and inaccurate accusations that all open-source licenses are unfriendly to commercial interests.

The EPL is *not* viral in nature. If you modify Eclipse with your own proprietary code and redistribute this new product, the Eclipse portion is still under the EPL. You must provide access to the recipients for the Eclipse portion; however, your code can still remain closed. You can still retain rights to your code.

This is another reason why Eclipse enjoys commercial support. The EPL was created to create commercial opportunities and yet remain free so that anyone can use it. Companies have created products using Eclipse as a base, and sold them commercially. IBM's WebSphere Studio products are a prime example. The WebSphere Studio family are IDEs with enterprise-friendly features such as UML diagramming support and J2EE tools built on top of Eclipse.

Being 'free' works very well with PHP. We now have a free tool to develop websites using a great, free language. With PHP and Eclipse/PHPeclipse, your development costs drop dramatically.

Eclipse Frees You from Vendor Lock-In

A more compelling consequence of the plug-in architecture is its meaning for open source in general. Development toolmakers want you to buy as many of their products as possible. They may hinder others from making IDEs for their proprietary language either by charging exorbitant licensing fees or taking a bully-like stand in enforcing patents. They may also offer tighter integration to their other tools while not giving the same access to other vendors. The more you adopt their closed technology, the more they can sell to you, and after time, the more expensive it will be to migrate out if you don't want to play with them any more.

Eclipse does not adopt this strategy. First and foremost, vendor lock-in is directly against the philosophy of the open-source community. Open-source software is all about giving users rights and freedoms. Second, due to the plug-in architecture, it's pretty much impossible to lock people in from a technical standpoint. No matter what the language, there's probably a plug-in for it, and if there isn't, you can always write one.

No longer are developers tied to one proprietary tool, product, or closed license. If you wish to develop in C# for .NET, you do not have to purchase Microsoft Visual Studio. You can just download one of the C# plug-ins for Eclipse. It is, quite blatantly, the open-source method of embrace and extend.

Finally, if you do not like the way a plug-in or Eclipse is working, you can always change it. The open-source license gives you the rights to modify Eclipse itself. Further, since many plug-ins are themselves open source, you can also modify them for your own use. You may even want to join the project and share your changes with the world.

Cross-Platform

The most basic requirement for Eclipse is having a computer with Java 1.4 installed and SWT. Both packages have been ported to most modern operating systems. Binaries of the Eclipse Platform are available for platforms such as Mac OS X, Windows XP, Linux (with Motif and GTK 2), Solaris, AIX, and HP-UX. Further, since plug-ins are also written in Java and SWT, most plug-ins are also cross-platform.

With Eclipse, application development is nearly operating-system agnostic. You can work on a project on an XP box at work, commit your changes, download the new code to your Apple Powerbook, and work from home. Programmers in the information technology department can work on a project using their Windows and Linux boxes while front-end HTML coders in marketing can use their Mac OS X machines to create web pages.

Professional Features

Out of the box, Eclipse has everything you would find in a commercial IDE. Features include a debugging environment, resource sharing, powerful search facility, and a syntax-aware text editor.

PHPEclipse

The PHPEclipse project was started to address two problems. First and foremost, it brought PHP functionality to the Eclipse platform. Second, as good as Eclipse is for Java application development, it had its shortcomings as a web development IDE. Anyone who has developed web applications using traditional editors like Macromedia's HomeSite or Bare Bones' BBEdit know the annoyance of constantly switching to external applications during development—dropping into Query Analyzer to connect to a database or constantly hitting *Refresh* in a web browser just to see if your CSS modifications work.

The PHPEclipse plug-in has addressed both issues admirably by focusing on what PHP web developers typically need to create an application. Started in 2002, PHPEclipse's development is active and its tool set provides everything that we need to write web applications in PHP.

The PHPEclipse package brings to Eclipse:

- An excellent PHP editor that knows about PHP syntax and built-in functions
- A debugger to help troubleshoot PHP code
- phpDocumentor, a tool like JavaDoc, which helps us quickly create documentation for our code
- An interface to SQL databases using the QuantumDB plug-in
- Tools for deployment to production servers via FTP, SFTP, WebDAV

There are other great PHP IDEs like NuSphere's PhpED and Zend's Zend Studio that are great at writing PHP applications. There is also another PHP plug-in for Eclipse—Xored's TruStudio. However, they too suffer from this same lack-of-integration drawback as the editors. None of these other packages comes with the breadth of external tools that PHPEclipse includes. Like Eclipse/PHPEclipse, you can write code quickly, but unlike Eclipse/PHPEclipse, you still need to use other programs to do other tasks. Most of all, Eclipse and PHPEclipse are free while the others require heavy licensing payments.

Summary

Eclipse is an IDE unlike any other. It is rare to find a product that enjoys fervent support from both major corporations and the open-source community. Eclipse, however, is one such product. Eclipse came about from IBM's development and its subsequent rallying of support from industry businesses. Its final handoff of Eclipse to a non-profit corporation has only enhanced Eclipse's potential. From the very first release, this free product was loaded with features that often cost thousands of dollars in other IDEs. The core philosophy of Eclipse is to be a tool to create other tools. It is often said that the Eclipse Platform is the ultimate tool to make tools. Its end-user license and architecture support this philosophy.

Taking advantage of this architecture is the PHPEclipse plug-in. Designed from the ground up to fulfill the needs of a PHP web developer, the combination of PHPEclipse and the Eclipse Platform gives everyone everything they would need to create web applications in a professional manner.

2
Installation

For development of client/server applications, we will need to have elements of both the client end and the server end. Obviously, we'll also need to install Eclipse itself and the additional software required for it. Finally, we will install the PHPEclipse plug-in to tie everything together.

For each software package, we will break down the requirements for installing on Mac OS X, Windows, and Linux platforms.

Installing Apache/PHP

We will need to turn our desktop machine into an Apache web server running PHP. This will take care of the server part of client/server. The goal is to simulate the production environment. By closely imitating the production environment, we will catch any problem before the program is released to the world.

Windows

The easiest way to install Apache and PHP on Windows is by using XAMPP project's XAMPP package. The XAMPP project packages Apache, MySQL, and PHP into one, easy-to-install directory. In addition, the XAMPP package installs FileZilla, FTP server and client, Mercury mail server, Webalizer web log analysis software, and phpMyAdmin—a web GUI to administer MySQL.

To install XAMPP, download it from the official XAMPP site at `http://www.apachefriends.org/en/xampp.html`. The XAMPP package comes in either as an installer, zip archive, or an executable self-extracting zip file. The installer is a quick and easy way to install XAMPP so we will recommend that you use this method to install XAMPP. By default, the installer will install everything; all the components (Apache, MySQL, PHP, etc.), in one directory named `xampp`.

XAMPP's Other Packages

For PHP development using Eclipse, all we need is the full XAMPP installer. However, the XAMPP project also includes several programming language add-ons and these are available on the XAMPP download page. If you ever need to run Perl, Python, or a Tomcat server, these XAMPP installers are an easy way to get them up and running quickly.

This directory contains the binary, configuration, web document, and startup files. Even though you could uninstall XAMPP by deleting this directory, if you want to uninstall it you should use the uninstaller. The XAMPP installer does make a few registry entries. Using the uninstaller ensures that everything is cleaned up correctly.

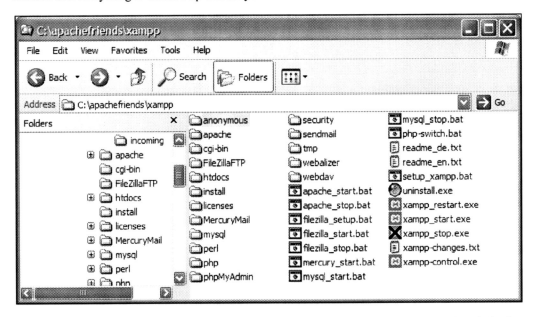

The system tray shortcut created by the installer is a link to the XAMPP control panel. This is also added as a shortcut in the Start menu. This Control Panel gives us a quick visual on which XAMPP services are currently running, and allows us to start and stop the services.

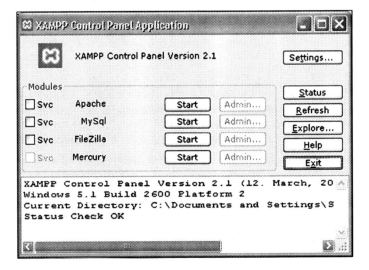

The XAMPP package also includes various scripts and .bat files to start and stop each service, but none offers one consolidated place to do everything, like we have with the control panel. We will invoke and use this control panel whenever we need services stopped and restarted. For now, we will need to start up Apache. Later on, use this control panel to start MySQL and FileZilla. Be aware that XAMPP installs Apache 2.0. Apache 1.3.x is still very popular in production environments. This should not affect PHP development, but be cognizant of this discrepancy. What may affect development is XAMPP's default version of PHP 5. If you are running version PHP 4 in production, you may be adversely affected since there are many features that are available in PHP 5 but not in PHP 4, and also the construct for objects is different in the two versions. If you need to switch, XAMPP includes the php-switch.bat utility located in the xampp directory. This utility automatically detects whether you are running PHP 4 or PHP 5, and switches to the other. To switch, simply double-click on the php-switch.bat file and confirm the change in the command-line screen that appears.

PHP keeps all its configuration settings in a file called php.ini. In order to do this switch, XAMPP keeps three versions of the php.ini file. There is one copy used in production, a template for PHP 4 that is copied over to production when you switch to PHP 4, and a template for PHP 5 that is copied over to production when you switch to PHP 5. If you do switch back and forth, you will need to make changes for all three, otherwise, your changes will disappear when you switch and the templates get copied over.

> The version used by the running version of PHP is the file \xampp\apache\bin\php.ini.
> The PHP 4 template is the file \xampp\php\php4\php4.ini.
> The PHP 5 template is the one at \xampp\php\php5.ini.

This is extremely important to remember in Chapter 5 when we install the debugger. In order to install the debugger, we will need to make some changes to our php.ini files. An alternative is to just make changes in the running version of our PHP, and not switch back and forth.

> The code examples used in this book assume you are running PHP 5. However, the sample application available for download also includes a version ported for PHP 4.

Mac OS X

Mac OS X has Apache already installed. We will download and install a separate package for PHP. To fully complete this process, you will need to be on an account with administrator rights.

To install PHP and turn on Apache, we will use Marc Liyanage's excellent PHP for Apache module package. Go to http://www.entropy.ch/software/macosx/php/ and download one of the packages available. If you are on Jaguar (Mac OS 10.2), the only version available is the one for PHP 4.3. For Panther (10.3) users, there is a package for PHP 5 and 4.3. While PHP 5 is newer, you should use whatever is closest to your production web environment.

Other Ways to Install PHP on Mac OS X

If you are using Panther (Mac OS 10.3) or greater, PHP 4.3 already comes installed. You could use that instead of Marc Liyanage's package. However, the native PHP build is relatively bare. Marc Liyanage's package includes many libraries that are not included with the native install. Moreover, Marc's package greatly simplifies installation. If you want to use the native PHP, you will have to go through turning on the root account, editing the Apache configuration file to make Apache aware of PHP, and then manually starting Apache.

XAMPP also includes a package for Mac OS X. However, the package, as of this writing, is in beta and lacks the GUI control panel included for Windows. If you do choose this route, some of the instructions we discuss may not work exactly on OS X as they do on Windows.

This package mounts as a disk image (.dmg) file. Double-click on this .dmg file and the image will mount. Open up this disk and you will find a .pkg file named php-*version*.pkg, where *version* is the PHP package version you downloaded.

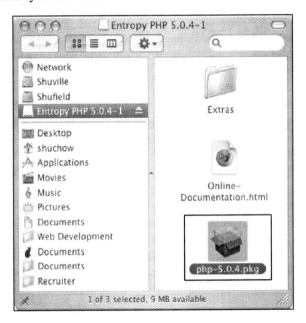

Double-click on this .pkg file and follow the instructions on screen. Install the package to your start-up hard drive. The installation script will turn on Personal Web Sharing in your Sharing control panel. This will turn on Apache and turn your Mac OS X machine into a web server. Should you ever want to turn off the web server, or if you ever need to restart Apache, check or uncheck the Personal Web Sharing checkbox.

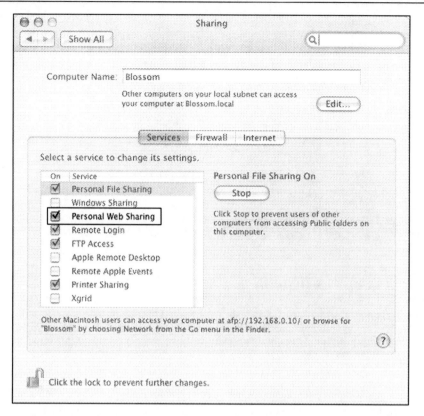

The same warning about XAMPP's versioning of Apache and PHP that we saw in Windows applies here. Marc Liyanage offers PHP 4.3 and PHP 5 packages, so you do have a choice. Mac OS X, however, only includes Apache 1.3. Source code as well as a binary of Apache 2 is available at http://apache.org/.

Linux

If you are installing under Linux, we will assume that you know what you are doing to a certain degree. Most Linux distributions include Apache and PHP at least as an optional installation, if not as standard default. If they are not installed, check your documentation for instructions on how to install using packages such as RPMs or .deb. You may also need to modify the Apache configuration file to make Apache aware of PHP's existence. Generally, you then start and stop Apache via the command line using the apachectl binary. Some distributions may also include control panels or administrative GUIs to control and configure Apache.

Alternatively, the XAMPP project also includes a package for Linux called XAMPP for Linux. You can download XAMPP for Linux and follow the same instructions as those for Windows.

Testing Apache

Using whichever instructions you followed for your operating system, start up the Apache web server. Launch your web browser and type in `http://localhost/` in the address bar. The web browser should request a page from Apache on your own computer that looks similar to the following:

This is the Apache test page. It is installed by default with all Apache installations. By requesting the default home page of `http://localhost/`, you have asked Apache to serve you this page. This tells us that Apache is alive and well on our machines. If you are using XAMPP you will also see a test default page, but it will look considerably different. The XAMPP Project has customized the XAMPP test page as seen in the screenshot overleaf.

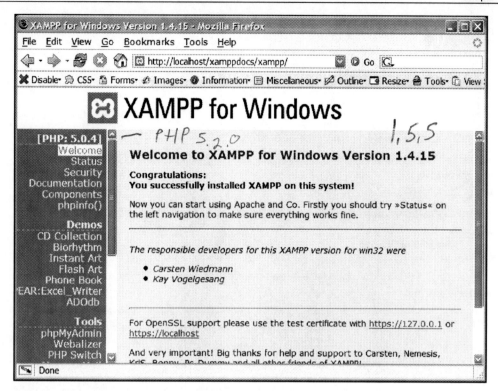

If the server times out, try using `http://127.0.0.1/` instead of `http://localhost/`. Also double-check if Apache is up and running.

Testing PHP

We will run a similar test to see if PHP is alive on our machine. To do so, we need to know the document root of our system. The document root is the directory where your website's files reside, including the Apache test page that we just saw.

If you followed the instructions so far, the document root for XAMPP users is `\xampp\htdocs\` and the one for Mac OS X is `/Library/WebServer/Documents/`. On Linux systems, open up a command-line terminal and type:

```
Buttercup:~ shuchow$ httpd -V
```

The settings that were compiled with Apache will be shown as output:

```
Server compiled with....
 -D EAPI
 -D HAVE_MMAP
 -D USE_MMAP_SCOREBOARD
 -D USE_MMAP_FILES
 -D HAVE_FCNTL_SERIALIZED_ACCEPT
 -D HAVE_FLOCK_SERIALIZED_ACCEPT
 -D SINGLE_LISTEN_UNSERIALIZED_ACCEPT
```

```
-D DYNAMIC_MODULE_LIMIT=64
-D HARD_SERVER_LIMIT=2048
-D HTTPD_ROOT="/usr"
-D SUEXEC_BIN="/usr/sbin/suexec"
-D DEFAULT_PIDLOG="/var/run/httpd.pid"
-D DEFAULT_SCOREBOARD="/var/run/httpd.scoreboard"
-D DEFAULT_LOCKFILE="/var/run/httpd.lock"
-D DEFAULT_ERRORLOG="/var/log/httpd/error_log"
-D TYPES_CONFIG_FILE="/etc/httpd/mime.types"
-D SERVER_CONFIG_FILE="/etc/httpd/httpd.conf"
-D ACCESS_CONFIG_FILE="/etc/httpd/access.conf"
-D RESOURCE_CONFIG_FILE="/etc/httpd/srm.conf"
```

Look for the `-D SERVER_CONFIG_FILE` line. The directory parameter points to the Apache configuration file in use. Open this file and search for 'DocumentRoot'. The directory after this is your document root.

In your document root directory, create a text file named `phpinfo.php` and type this in the file:

```
<?php
    phpinfo();
?>
```

The `phpinfo()` function will return and output a table of diagnostics about your PHP installation. You should see this:

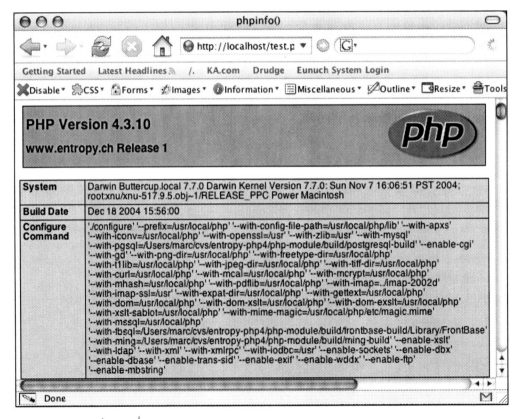

visible at
http://localhost/xampp/phpinfo.php

If you followed the directions for XAMPP (for Windows and Linux) or Marc Liyanage's package, this should work. If you just see your PHP code, for any operating system, then the Apache web server is not configured to pass .php files to the PHP parser before serving them. Open your Apache configuration file; chances are there are these two lines:

```
#LoadModule php4_module          libexec/httpd/libphp4.so
```
and

```
#AddModule mod_php4.c
```

The hash symbol at the beginning means that the lines are commented out, and thus, Apache was not told about PHP's presence. Remove the hash symbols and restart Apache.

Installing Java

Since Eclipse is a Java application, we will need a Java Runtime Environment (JRE). You may already have a runtime environment, especially if you have installed the **Java Development Kit (JDK)**. If you have a JRE or the JDK, you can skip this section.

The runtime environment is the engine that allows you to run Java applications. The JDK includes the runtime environment and has tools that let you create and compile Java programs. Even if you do not program in Java right now, as a developer, you should install the JDK. You may want to program in Java or JSP down the road. The instructions below will guide you on how to download the JDK.

Windows

You can download the official JDK at http://java.sun.com/j2se/corejava/index.jsp. Click on the link for the latest version and follow the links to download the JDK for your platform. The site also maintains a list of popular downloads in the right navigation bar. The list includes a direct link to the latest JDK download pages. You need to find the correct link for your platform.

For Windows, the download will come in the form of an installer. Once the installer has completed, execute it and follow the instructions of the installation wizard. The installer will install all necessary files and automatically configure the workstation.

> A note about Sun's Java versioning: Java 1.1 and below are simply known as Java. Java 2 is the marketing name for Java 1.2 through 1.4. When 1.5 was released, Sun christened it Java 5. Eclipse requires at least Java 2 but Java 5 will also work fine. You may also see references to J2EE (Java 2, Enterprise Edition) and J2ME (Micro Edition). For our purposes, we need at least J2SE, (Java 2, Standard Edition). Simple and clear, isn't it?

Mac OS X

Mac OS X comes with Java 2 installed and configured by default. There is nothing more we need to do.

Linux

Again, your distribution may include Java as an installation option. If not, go to the official Sun site at http://java.sun.com/j2se/corejava/index.jsp and follow the link to download the latest JDK for your platform. Accept the licensing agreement and click on the link for the Linux platform. An RPM package is available for distributions that support Red Hat RPMs. Double-click on the downloaded file to install.

Some installations of Linux will install a Java clone. This has been known to cause problems with Eclipse. For this reason, it is recommended that you install the official Sun distribution of Java.

Testing Java

To test Java on any platform, open up a command (DOS) prompt window (if you're on Windows) or a terminal (if you're on Mac OS X or Linux) and type:

```
Buttercup:~ shuchow$ java -version
```

The java command will invoke Java and the -version parameter will tell it to output general information about the Java installation including version number.

```
java version "1.4.2_05"
Java(TM) 2 Runtime Environment, Standard Edition (build 1.4.2_05-141.3)
Java HotSpot(TM) Client VM (build 1.4.2-38, mixed mode)
```

If you get a 'command not found' error, try re-running the Java installer. You may have Java classpaths set up incorrectly, which the installer should fix.

If you are still having problems with installation, you can get help at the Sun community forums at http://forum.java.sun.com/index.jspa. There are many helpful topics including some geared towards installation issues.

Eclipse

Now it is time to actually obtain and install Eclipse. The installation process is the same for all major platforms.

Downloading Eclipse

Eclipse's download page is at http://www.eclipse.org/downloads/index.php. This is the main download gateway page to all projects of the Eclipse Foundation, including the Eclipse Project itself. Each project has its own section on this page. The download options can be a little daunting, so we'll explain everything.

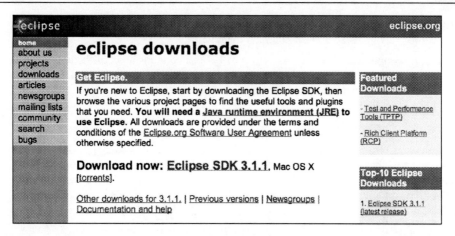

The simplest and fastest way to get Eclipse up and running is to download the latest release of the Eclipse Platform SDK. To do this, simply click on the link to the Eclipse SDK version. From there, you will be taken to a list of mirrors based on geographic location. Pick a mirror close to you and click on the link. This will start the download of a zip archive of the Eclipse SDK.

You can find Eclipse downloads for other operating systems, source code, documentation, or just individual components of the platform (remember that everything is a plug-in in Eclipse) under the Other Downloads for… link. Clicking on this link will take you to a page with download links for all of the supported operating systems; this page also contains the source code. Underneath this are links to the official Eclipse Platform documentation. Following that are links to individual plug-ins like the JDT, PDE, and SWT.

If you are feeling bold, nostalgic, or worldly, you can download previous and bleeding edge versions of the SDK and language packs. From the eclipse downloads page, go to the Eclipse Project section and click on Downloads.

The eclipse project downloads page first lists the most popular downloads for the project. The latest release is listed first. Future releases are listed after that, and finally the most recent old version is available. There are several types of builds available on the eclipse downloads page:

Use This

- **Release Build**: Release builds are those that are deemed ready for the whole world to use. Releases get a version number and are the most tested and stable versions available. Every major version of Eclipse is available here.
- **Stable Build**: The next version of Eclipse is available in Stable Builds. They are pulled from integration builds after a few days of informal testing and usage by Eclipse developers. Stable builds often have new features and new bugs. They are released in order to be tested. If you are going to use the stable build, you can help make Eclipse better by reporting any bugs you find back to the Eclipse development team.
- **Integration Build**: Integration builds are the development progress of individual components of the Platform. When a stable build is created, it takes the latest integration build from each component. They are built whenever a component releases a new version into the main platform build. We should not worry about integration builds as they are only an interesting artifact of the Eclipse development process.

27

- **Nightly Build**: Nightly builds are snapshots of source code every night. They are completely untested and often do not even work.

- **Maintenance Build**: If a new version of Eclipse contains most of the bug fixes for the most current version, it is released as a maintenance build. The Eclipse development team has tested the bug fixes among themselves.

- **Language Pack**: Language packs are available for every release version of Eclipse to make it accessible and usable worldwide.

For our purposes, we'll just play it safe and use the latest release build for all of our development. Also keep in mind that many third-party plug-ins, including PHPEclipse, are not officially supported when used in stable builds. Then again, by using them in stable builds, you can help these plug-in developers by reporting compatibility issues with their plug-ins and contribute to future Eclipse releases.

Installing Eclipse

The process of installing Eclipse is merely unzipping the SDK zip file you've downloaded and moving it into your favorite applications or programs directory. There is no need to walk through installers, no modification of registry settings, no system environment variable changes, no placement of hidden files in obscure locations, and no rebooting required.

Open the eclipse directory:

There are several directories and things to note here:

- The actual Eclipse program is in this directory with the Eclipse icon.

- startup.jar is a special launcher used by Eclipse.

- There are HTML files here and more in the readme directory. These are legal notices and information about the Eclipse license.

- The configuration directory holds settings used by the runtime environment. Any setting changes are held in here. If this directory is deleted, the runtime will create a new one at Eclipse's launch, but your settings will be reset to their defaults.

- The plugins directory holds all plug-ins used by eclipse including all core plug-ins like the JDT and PDE. All third-party plug-ins will also be stored in here including PHPEclipse. Each plug-in comprises one or more subdirectories. They hold the compiled binary code of the plug-in and all settings and manifest files used by the plug-in.

- The features directory is used by some plug-ins. Features are the grouping and packaging of plug-ins. A feature does not carry any binary code. The main part of a feature is a definition file of what plug-ins go together. An example of a feature in this directory is the JDT. The JDT is defined in the feature as comprising of the editor, debugger, and console. Not all plug-ins have features, but PHPEclipse does.

There are subdirectories in the plugins and features directories, each beginning with 'org' or 'net'. Eclipse plug-ins are given a technical name that follows Java packaging standards. This standard is based on the internet **Domain Name System (DNS)**, with the name of the plug-in having the same high-level name as the organization that develops it. Since most of the Eclipse SDK's plug-ins are from the Eclipse Foundation, most plug-ins begin with 'org.eclipse'. However, Eclipse comes bundled with Ant, an Apache project. Therefore, that plug-in's name begins with 'org.apache.ant'. This system greatly reduces the chances of naming conflicts and gives us a good idea of who is responsible for a plug-in.

An individual plug-in's binary code, configuration files, and licenses are stored within these directories.

Installing PHPEclipse

Finally, we will install the last component we need—the PHPEclipse plug-in. We need to grab the plug-in itself from the PHPEclipse site at SourceForge.

Historically, PHPEclipse was installed by unzipping an archive of directories and manually moving them into the plug-ins or features directory. The most recent versions of PHPEclipse, however, let us use the Eclipse update manager to handle the installation. In these instructions, we will use the historical method to install Eclipse since it is important to understand how the Eclipse plug-in directories work with each other. Also, going through this method introduces us to the official PHPEclipse site and the project site on SourceForge. If you wish to install with the newer method via the update manager, full instructions and walkthroughs are available in Appendix B.

> PHPEclipse is a SourceForge project. SourceForge is a site that offers free communication and collaboration tools to the development teams of open-source projects. Among SourceForge's services is to host files for the project. Note that this site is different from the official PHPEclipse site at `http://www.phpeclipse.de`. The official site is targeted at PHPEclipse end users, and thus, has a more varied community, while the PHPEclipse SourceForge site is more geared for developers.

To download the files, visit the official SourceForge site at `http://sourceforge.net/projects/phpeclipse`. Click on the link to Files.

You can also arrive at the SourceForge site by going to the official PHPEclipse site at `http://www.phpeclipse.de`, and clicking on Downloadable Files in the left navigation bar.

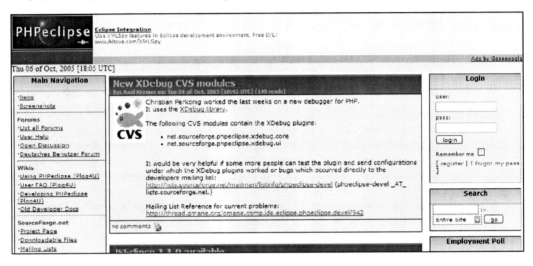

At the SourceForge file downloads area, you will see all the files available for download from a project. This usually includes current releases, historic releases, beta and alpha versions, any auxiliary files, and source code. Releases are grouped by Eclipse compatibility streams. PHPEclipse releases grouped in Eclipse 2.1 will only work with Eclipse 2.1, and releases in the Eclipse 3.0 stream will only work with Eclipse versions 3.0.x, and so forth.

Package	Release & Notes	Filename	Date			
			Size	D/L	Arch.	Type
phpeclipse (CVS snaphots) [show only this package]						
phpeclipse-1.1.8-cvs-20051006 [show only this release]			**2005-10-06 09:41**			
Download net.sourceforge.phpeclipse_1.1.8.bin.dist.zip			9662217	0	Platform-Independent	.zip
phpeclipse (Eclipse2.1 stream) [show only this package]						
src-snapshot-213-RC1 [show only this release]			**2004-01-27 15:00**			
Download src-snapshot-eclipse213-ide.zip			6830071	12820	Platform-Independent	.zip
bin-snapshot-wampp2-RC1 [show only this release]			**2004-01-19 15:00**			
Download bin-snapshot-wampp2-RC1.zip			7816173	7750	Platform-Independent	.zip
phpeclipse (Eclipse3.0 stream) [show only this package]						
phpeclipse-1.1.4-features [show only this release]			**2005-05-27 11:38**			
Download PHPeclipse-1.1.4-features.zip			22060927	41855	Platform-Independent	.zip
PHPEclipse1.1.3-2005-01-29 [show only this release]			**2005-01-29 03:52**			
Download PHPEclipse1.1.3-2005-01-29.zip			11217215	80874	Platform-Independent	.zip
PHPEclipse1.1.2-2004-12-04 [show only this release]			**2004-12-04 03:38**			
Download net.sourceforge.phpeclipse.webbrowser_1.1.2_linux.zip			253858	939	Platform-Independent	.zip

We are interested in the most recent release, for our stream, so click on the link that says, PHPEclipse-*Version-Date*-.zip where *Version-Date* is the most current date under the appropriate version of Eclipse that you downloaded. Clicking on this link will take you to a list of official SourceForge mirrors. Click on a file icon under the Downloads column from a mirror site geographically near you.

SOURCEFORGE™ .net

SOURCEFORGE.NET
DOWNLOAD
S E R V E R

You are requesting file: /phpeclipse/PHPeclipse-1.1.4-features.zip
Please select a mirror

Host	Location	Continent	Download
SURFnet	Amsterdam, The Netherlands	Europe	21544 kb
easynews	Phoenix, AZ	North America	21544 kb
OPTUS*net*	Sydney, Australia	Australia	21544 kb
UNIVERSITY OF KENT UK**MIRROR** service	Kent, UK	Europe	21544 kb
	Minneapolis, MN	North America	21544 kb
HEAnet	Dublin, Ireland	Europe	21544 kb
NCHC	Tainan, Taiwan	Asia	21544 kb

Your file should automatically begin downloading. It will come in as a zip file. Uncompress it to create a directory of the same name. Open this directory to reveal two folders: plugins and features.

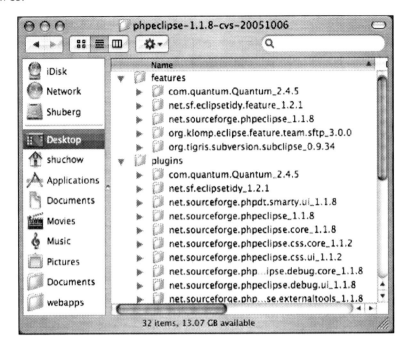

The directory structure is designed to mimic the directory structure of Eclipse. In other words, everything in the PHPEclipse plugins directory should be placed in the Eclipse plugins directory, and everything in this features directory should be placed in the Eclipse features directory. Like the Eclipse features and plugins directories, the one item under features directory defines what makes up the PHPEclipse package as a whole, while everything under plugins directory is the actual binary code for things like the debugger core and the web browser.

You'll notice that most of the items in the PHPEclipse package begin with net.sourceforge.phpeclipse. This follows the plug-in naming convention outlined earlier, since PHPEclipse is a SourceForge project, whose site is underneath the .net domain. If PHPEclipse was a commercial plug-in, we'd expect it to begin with com. Looking at the names of the directories, we get a hint of what features are available in PHPEclipse.

To install PHPEclipse, simply drag the directory contents into their respective directories in the Eclipse application directory.

Warning: Do not actually replace those directories.

For example, in the `features` directory, `net.sourceforge.phpeclipse-`*`version`* should go in
`...`*`Path_To_Eclipse`*`/features`. After you've moved them, the `features` and `plugins` directories
under eclipse should have a hodge-podge of directories beginning with `net.` and `org.`

Putting It All Together

Now, launch the Eclipse application. If you jumped ahead and launched Eclipse earlier, you will
have to quit and restart Eclipse in order for it to recognize the new PHPEclipse plug-in. Plug-ins
are only read once—when Eclipse starts up. To do a quick test of the PHPEclipse plug-in, go to
Window | Open Perspective | Other... and select the PHP option, then click the OK button. You
should see a set of XAMPP and Apache buttons along the top. These were installed by
PHPEclipse, and are a sign that everything was installed correctly.

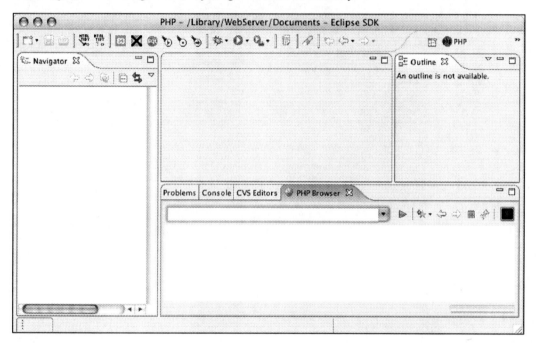

Summary

At this point, we have everything we need to write PHP applications. Web application
development is, in essence, a form of client/server development. By installing a fully functioning
version of Apache and PHP on our machines, we have created a server environment that
(hopefully) closely mirrors our environment in production. Since Eclipse is written in Java, we
need a Java Virtual Machine on our systems. Using Eclipse and PHPEclipse, we can now begin
writing applications for this server environment.

Later on, we will cover more advanced topics like debugging and database interaction. These
chapters will require more software to be installed, and we will also walk through those
installations when relevant. For now, though, we can start using Eclipse.

3
The Eclipse Interface

If you've never used an IDE, the Eclipse interface can be a bit daunting. Worse, if you've never used an IDE and have never programmed in Java, the Java-centric nature of Eclipse can make the initial screen downright intimidating.

Fortunately, the basic Eclipse philosophy is very logical and rather simple. In this chapter, we will walk through the startup process, explain the overall layout of Eclipse, and prepare Eclipse for PHP development. In particular, we will cover the following components and see how to maximize their use:

- Perspectives
- Views

For the next two chapters, we will use an example of an 'animal shelter' website. Most shelter websites have an inventory of pets available for adoption. We will create a sample web application to show this inventory.

Starting Eclipse

To start Eclipse, double-click on the Eclipse application icon in your file system. You will be presented with the Workspace Launcher, a dialog box asking you to select your workspace. Remember, the workspace is the part of Eclipse that manages application resources—things like source code files and graphics.

Immediately, we encounter a default Java-centric behavior of Eclipse that we will have to change. If we were creating regular Java applications, we would not care about Apache. Java code can be compiled at one location and the final binary files can be deployed at another location. Java source code does not need to be served by a web server, and thus, we can accept the default location that the workspace launcher presents. In multi-user workstations, we may change the location to a place underneath our user directory. Again, this is not a location accessible by our web server.

However, in PHP and web development, the location of our code matters. Apache serves the web pages, and it can only access certain areas in our file system. We need to be able to see our post-processed files. If we tell the application to echo out a variable, we need to use a web browser to request the file from a web server. The web server then sends the file to the PHP parser to determine the variable value, and finally back to the browser. Imagine the hassle it would be to make a one-line change to a page and then have to move it out to an area that Apache can access. If you made a mistake, you would have to repeat the whole process. It would be simpler to put the source code in the place from which Apache serves web pages.

The location where we put Apache's web pages is known as the document root location. We were introduced to document root in Chapter 2 when we tested our PHP installation. By using the document root as the workspace location, we are essentially placing our source code in an area that can be served. The document root location is defined in the Apache configuration file, httpd.conf. Assuming you followed the Apache/PHP installation instructions in the previous chapter, here again are the document root locations:

- **Windows**: \xampp\htdocs
- **Mac OS X**: /Library/WebServer/Documents
- **Linux**: Check your httpd.conf file or your distribution's documents.
  /var/www/html is a fairly common location used by Linux distributions.

You are not married to one workspace location in Eclipse. Notice that the Workspace location is a pull-down menu. Eclipse will remember the last few workspace locations you use. Further, you can individually override each project's location. If you use Eclipse for non-web application development, it may be wise, from a security standpoint, to put these other source files at a location not accessible by Apache, like your home directory or anywhere else outside your document root.

The Eclipse Welcome Screen

When you start Eclipse 3.x for the first time, you will be greeted with the Eclipse welcome screen:

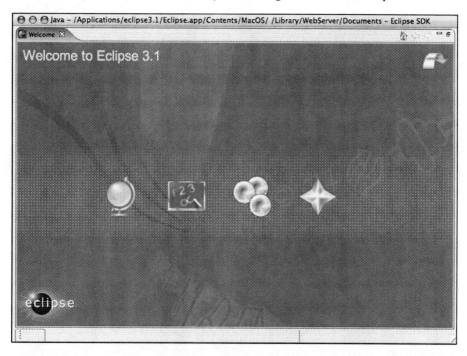

This page has a series of informational links to the integrated Eclipse help files. Most of these help screens are related to application development in Java or using Java to extend Eclipse. They won't be immediately important to our needs. However, after you've had a little hands-on experience with Eclipse, you may find it helpful and interesting to look through some of the screens to get a better understanding of how Eclipse works:

- **Overview:** This section gives a broad overview of Eclipse. It covers the Workbench, how to write Java with Eclipse, using CVS, and an introduction to plug-in development.

- **Tutorials:** Four tutorials are included in Eclipse: building a Java application, building an SWT application, building a plug-in, and deploying a plug-in.

- **Samples:** Some sample plug-in project files are linked from here. You will need an Internet connection to download the sample files.

- **What's New:** If you have used a previous version of Eclipse, this section will outline what has changed with this version of Eclipse. Also included are links to Eclipse community sites and instructions for migrating over older Eclipse Projects.

This welcome feature operates like a web browser. You can click on links and navigate between pages and to the home welcome screen using the navigation buttons in the upper right corner of the window.

For now, click the Workbench icon you see in the upper right corner to go directly to the Workbench. You can return to this screen at any time by selecting Help | Welcome from the main menu.

Perspectives

When you first launch Eclipse, you will be presented with this window:

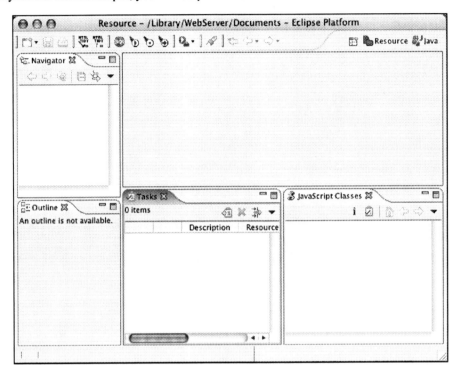

The Eclipse interface comprises a specific grouping of tabs in a window. Across the top are the main toolbar and the shortcut toolbar. The main menu will either be above the main toolbar if you are on Windows and Linux or above the window title if you are on Macintosh systems.

In Eclipse, tabs are called **views**. A view has one specific function. A special tab that is used to edit a resource is called an **editor**. Editors are used to write and edit source code.

A predefined layout of views and editors is called a **perspective**. Each perspective is geared towards a specific task or purpose. Java development has a perspective, debugging has a perspective, and so on. The PHPEclipse plug-in gives us a PHP perspective.

The developers of a plug-in collect all the views you need to do your tasks into a perspective. For example, the Java perspective gives us a view of all the methods in a class, a Java editor, a console, and an object hierarchy viewer, while the PHP perspective gives us a file system navigator, an HTML editor, a view of all functions in our application, a system console, and a web browser.

The perspective that you first encounter is the Resource perspective. It is the most generic of all perspectives. It has a general-purpose text editor and a file system browser. You can think of this as the home perspective. If you try to open a file that Eclipse does not recognize, it will try to open it in the Resource perspective.

Changing Perspectives

To change tasks, you often have to change perspectives. There are two ways to change perspectives in Eclipse.

Often, actions have perspectives associated with them. To change perspectives, you simply have to do an action that triggers a change. For example, if you are writing PHP code and wish to debug the application, Eclipse will automatically switch you to the Debug perspective when you initiate the debugging process.

The second way to switch perspectives is to manually change the perspective. In the shortcut toolbar, click on the Open Perspective icon located in the upper right corner:

You will get a pull-down menu of the most commonly used perspectives for Java development. To see all of the perspectives, select the Other... option in the pull-down menu:

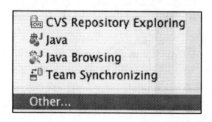

This will open the Select Perspective window:

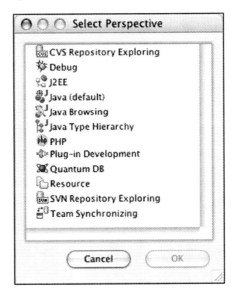

You can also open this window by selecting Window | Open Perspective | Other... from the main menu.

To change perspectives, select the desired perspective and click the OK button.

After installing the PHPEclipse plug-in, you should have the PHP and Quantum DB perspectives available. The other perspectives listed on this window are the default perspectives included with the Eclipse Platform and JDT downloads. If you install more plug-ins, they will also be available here.

Briefly, here are the functions of each perspective:

- CVS Repository Exploring: Used to browse CVS repositories. This plug-in will be covered in Chapter 7 where we explore CVS.

- Team Synchronizing: Another CVS perspective. For complex projects with a lot of branching, this plug-in helps specify where in the source-code tree a file should be uploaded.

- Debug: Debugging perspective used in both the Java and PHP development environments. PHP debugging will be covered in Chapter 5.

- Java (default): The primary perspective for Java development. Installed by the JDT.

- Java Type Hierarchy: Part of the JDT. Used to view the Java inheritance hierarchy of a Java project.

- Java Browsing: Part of the JDT. Used to view all of the packages and classes in all of the Java projects in your workspace.

- Plug-in Development: Used for developing plug-ins for Eclipse. Installed by the PDE.

- Resource: The default perspective.

- PHP: The main PHP development perspective. This is installed by the PHPEclipse plug-in.
- Quantum DB: The command-line SQL database interface installed by the Quantum DB plug-in as part of the PHPEclipse package. The use of this plug-in is covered in Chapter 6.

Change Your Default Perspective

By default, Eclipse will open the Java perspective. If you are going to use Eclipse mostly for PHP development, you can change the default perspective by going to the Window | Preferences | General | Perspectives menu option. Choose the PHP perspective and click on the Make Default button.

As you open perspectives, they will appear as options in the shortcut toolbar for easier access in future. You can remove the perspectives that you do not need from this toolbar by right-clicking on the perspective and selecting Close. You can also fit more perspectives in this toolbar by resizing it. Drag the left border of the toolbar to resize it.

Once you have several perspectives activated, you can cycle through them in the main menu using Window | Navigation | Next Perspective or Previous Perspective.

Quantum DB Perspective

The Quantum DB perspective will be covered in depth in Chapter 6. We mention it here since it is one of three perspectives installed by PHPEclipse.

The Quantum DB plug-in, as part of PHPEclipse, installs this perspective. PHP SQL interfaces with databases using a JDBC driver. In this perspective, you can write SQL statements directly against the database. If you send a SELECT command, you can see the data returned directly to you in a view. Using Quantum DB, you no longer have to jump into a separate application to retrieve or manipulate data from a database. You can even alter and maintain the database right from Eclipse.

In Chapter 6, we will walk through installation, configuration, and usage of this powerful plug-in.

Editors

Editors are used to edit or create a resource. Generally, in any language development perspective, a large space is reserved for documents opened in an editor. In this book, we will encounter three editors—the PHP editor, the Quantum SQL editor, and the generic text editor featured in the Resource perspective.

The differences between the three are subtle because the former two leverage and extend the generic editor. Even JDT's Java editor operates in the same way. This makes the appearance of each editor fairly similar to the end user—all three appear to be simple text editors. The only real differences are features that need to be customized for each language, like syntax highlighting and keyword alerts.

Editors are invoked when you open a document either by double-clicking on the file or selecting an external file to open using the File | Open File... option. The Workbench chooses the appropriate editor based on a particular order:

1. The editor that last opened the file.
2. The file extension of the resource. Later, we will see how to edit these extension-editor associations in the Preferences menu option.
3. Any external application defined by the operating system based on the file extension.
4. Finally, if all else fails, Eclipse will try to open the file using the Resource perspective's default editor.

PHPEclipse Views

From a GUI standpoint, views are the individual tabs seen in the Workbench. Functionally, views offer information and resources taken from external and local systems relevant to the developer. In other words, if you need information to develop an application, a view interfaces with these entities to provide you with that information. If you need information from your local file system, an FTP server, a database, or even the application itself, this information is grabbed and presented by a view.

The various plug-ins installed by the Eclipse Platform give us many views for Java development. We will, however, concentrate only on the views from the PHP perspective. Similar to the perspectives, you can manually show all available views using the Window | Show View | Other... menu option. This will open the Show View window:

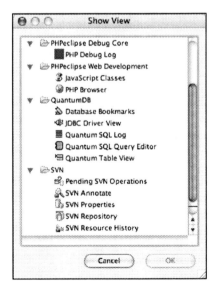

Click a desired view and click the OK button to open the view. This window shows which plug-in belongs to which view.

Navigator View

The Navigator view is one of the most important views of Eclipse. The view interfaces with local and remote file systems to show you all of the files associated with an application. To understand how the Navigator view works, we need to understand how Eclipse organizes applications.

In Eclipse, each application is a project. A project comprises files and subdirectories. A file can be anything needed by the application—source code, graphics, Java JAR files, etc. The Navigator view reflects your file system. When you create a project (which we will walk through in the next chapter), a directory of the same name is created under the workspace you specify. As you add directories, source code, and project files to your project in the Navigator view, the files are also created under your workspace.

However, the Navigator view does not synchronize in real time with the file system. If you add files to the workspace's area in the file system via the operating system, the Navigator view will not know about these files. Conversely, if you delete files in the workspace outside of Eclipse, the Navigator view is not aware of the deletions and Eclipse will throw an error if it tries to access these missing files. If any changes are made to the workspace outside of Eclipse, you can synchronize Eclipse and the file system by clicking on the project in question and selecting File | Refresh in the main menu.

The Navigator view operates similarly to a typical file directory browser in most operating systems. The triangles beside the directories collapse or expand the tree. You can drag and drop files into directories and other projects. You can also set the Navigator to show only a directory or project by clicking on the resource and selecting Navigate | Go Into in the main menu. From there, you can use the toolbar buttons at the top of the view to navigate through the hierarchy.

Back: Moves to the Navigator view previously selected. If you were viewing the whole workspace and selected Go Into a project, you will return to the workspace.

 Forward: Moves forward to the view in the Navigator. After selecting Back in the previous example, clicking the Forward button will return you to the project you were in previously.

 Up: Moves up one level in the Navigator view with the top level being the workspace. In the sample workspace shown before, if you were in the styles directory, clicking Up once will take you to the ShelterSite level. Clicking Up again will take you to the workspace.

 Collapse All: Collapses all expanded directories and projects. This is a standard icon that you will see in most views that display and organize things in a tree-like fashion.

 Link with Editor: If a file is selected in an editor, clicking this button will highlight the file in the navigator schema. This is a common feature of views that are directly related to files being edited in an editor.

 Menu: The Menu is a pull-down menu that features tools to control the display of the Navigator view. This is a standard item that you will see in almost all the views. Clicking on this icon will bring up other options specific to the view.

The Navigator view's Menu houses the working sets options, sorting options, and the filtering tools.

Working Sets

The navigator view also features a powerful selection mechanism. This feature allows you to define sets of documents in your workspace and show them in the view. To define a working set, choose Select Working Set... in the menu:

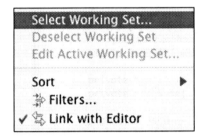

This will bring up the Select Working Set window:

If you have not created any previous working sets, this window will be blank. Otherwise, you can edit or delete your existing working sets from here. In this example, a working set named Dogs has been created. We'll create a new one for felines named Cats. Click the New... button to create a working set:

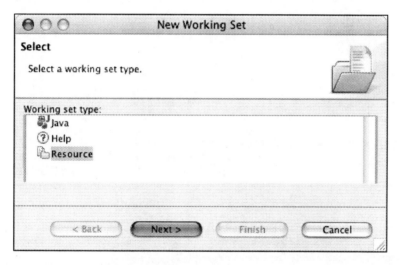

In this example, we'll select Resource as our working set type. This will allow us to select source code files from the workspace. Java working sets would work, but are overkill for our purposes. They are like Resource sets, but include the ability to drill into JAR files. Help working sets allow you to select help documentation included in Eclipse for quick and easy access.

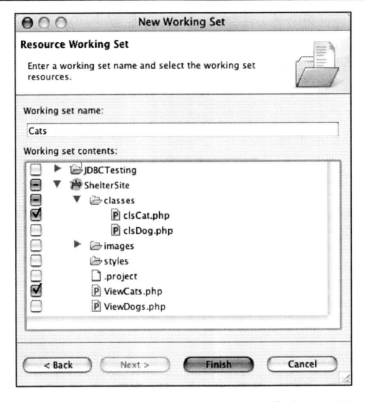

Suppose we wanted to view only the pages in our application that display cats. We give the working set the name Cats and we can traverse the workspace marking only the pages that are relevant. All of our projects and files are available for selection here, you will see a blank screen as we haven't added any files yet. Working sets are not limited to one project nor are files and directories limited to one working set.

Once we create a working set, it is automatically selected in the Navigator view. All the other files and directories in the workspace are hidden from view. To show all files again, go back to the Navigator view Menu and select Deselect Working Set...

As you define more working sets, they will appear in the Menu, allowing you to quickly switch back and forth between sets.

Console View

The console view interacts with system messages. System errors and output are displayed in the console. The console view is installed by the JDT, but used by PHPEclipse. More than one plug-in utilizes the console view. Therefore, even though there is only one visible console, there can be several hidden consoles. This is very similar to tabs in modern browsers. PHPeclipse uses the console shown next:

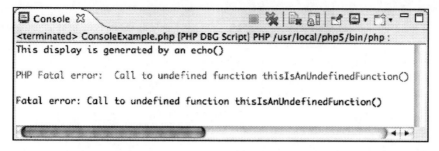

The console view toolbar controls the behavior of the console when running a particular process. The various tools available are listed in the following table (some of them are activated only after you have opened a project in Eclipse):

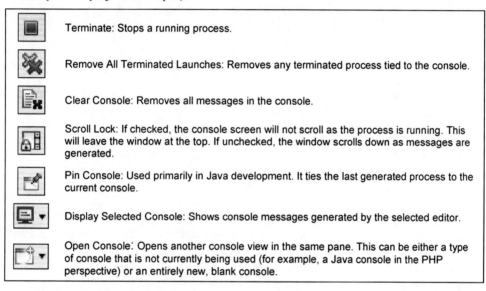

■	Terminate: Stops a running process.
✳	Remove All Terminated Launches: Removes any terminated process tied to the console.
▤✖	Clear Console: Removes all messages in the console.
🔒	Scroll Lock: If checked, the console screen will not scroll as the process is running. This will leave the window at the top. If unchecked, the window scrolls down as messages are generated.
✎	Pin Console: Used primarily in Java development. It ties the last generated process to the current console.
▣ ▼	Display Selected Console: Shows console messages generated by the selected editor.
▤ ▼	Open Console: Opens another console view in the same pane. This can be either a type of console that is not currently being used (for example, a Java console in the PHP perspective) or an entirely new, blank console.

In PHP, output is generated by the echo() or print() functions. Error messages are generated anytime the PHP interpreter encounters an error. The color, display, and behavior of the console can be controlled in the Eclipse Preferences window by selecting Window | Preferences in the main menu. From there, select Run/Debug | Console.

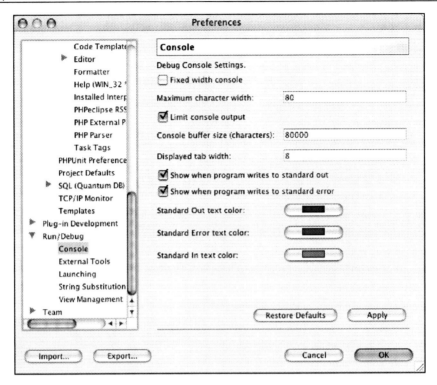

Problems View

The Problems view reports coding errors in an orderly and comprehensive fashion. The editors of a language typically leverage the Problems view for error reporting. When a syntax error in the language is detected, it is reported in this view.

Again, the Problems view reports errors in the code that we write. It does not report Eclipse runtime errors. In Chapter 5, on debugging, we will use another view, the Error Log view, to see runtime problems with Eclipse and PHPEclipse.

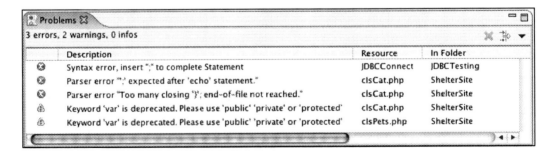

The Problems view reports errors on all files in the workspace regardless of the perspective you are using. This view only has two icons plus a Menu pulldown:

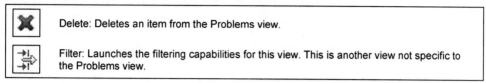

Delete: Deletes an item from the Problems view.

Filter: Launches the filtering capabilities for this view. This is another view not specific to the Problems view.

In the screenshot above, we see not only PHP errors from a PHP project, but also a syntax error in a Java project. We can filter the view itself with the filter icon in the toolbar. With the filter, we can tell the Problems view to reduce the types of items shown. We can filter by project type, resource, and by words and phrases in the Description.

A filter only masks what is shown. We also have some control over the error levels actually reported in the Problems view. To change these reporting levels, go to the Windows | Preferences | PHPEclipse Web Development | PHP | PHP Parser menu option. The PHP Parser's preferences features are inherited from the JDT. Therefore, any changes to them will trigger a dialog box that warns you that a full rebuild is required. Even though builds are not relevant in PHP projects, if you do make any changes, click the Yes button to accept this rebuild.

This describes only the filtering capabilities of the Problems view. Other views that utilize filtering will have their own options that are relevant to that view.

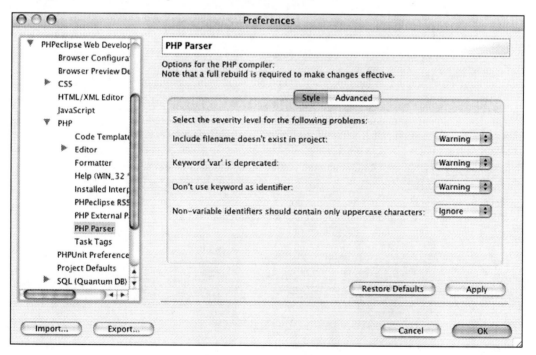

Outline View

The Outline view is designed to give the developer a complete view of a page's functions and properties. In Java, the properties and methods of a class would be listed. In procedural PHP, a script's user-defined functions would be shown. Like Java, in object-oriented PHP, the properties of a class would also be listed. In Java, the Outline view also gives the developer visual hints of a method's access modifiers based on icons. With PHP 5, the syntax differences between object-oriented PHP and Java have greatly diminished. Concepts such as static variables and public, private, and protected access modifiers are now available in PHP. This has made the Outline view behave similarly for both languages.

Consider a sample class of a cat at an animal shelter. A very basic PHP 5 class could look like this:

```php
<?php
  class Cat
  {
    static $ADDRESS = "6201 Florin-Perkins Road";
    private $catID;
    private $catName;

    public function getCatID($id)
    {
      //code
    }

    public function setCatID($id)
    {
      //code
    }

    private function getSpeciesID($id)
    {
      //code
    }

    protected function getCatBreed($id)
    {
      //code
    }
  }
?>
```

Our feline has three properties. Since the address of the cat will not change (as the address is the shelter's address itself), the ADDRESS variable is static. The two private variables are the ID and the name. We have created public get and set functions for the ID of the cat. There is a protected function to get the breed of the cat and a private function to get the species ID.

In the Outline view, this code would look like this:

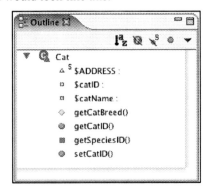

The name of the class is shown and the structure is collapsible via the triangle icon. The shape and color of the icon tell you whether the item is a function or a variable and the access modifier. Red squares are private items, yellow diamonds are protected items, and green circles are public items. If the icon is a solid shape, it is a function, while a smaller, hollow shape denotes a variable.

In PHP 4, with more rudimentary object-oriented features, properties and functions are treated as if they had the `public` modifier.

The toolbar menu for the Outline view controls filtering and how the information is displayed:

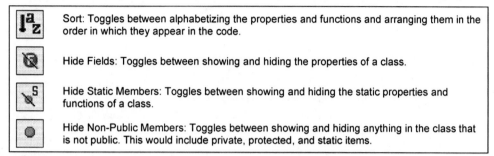

	Sort: Toggles between alphabetizing the properties and functions and arranging them in the order in which they appear in the code.
	Hide Fields: Toggles between showing and hiding the properties of a class.
	Hide Static Members: Toggles between showing and hiding the static properties and functions of a class.
	Hide Non-Public Members: Toggles between showing and hiding anything in the class that is not public. This would include private, protected, and static items.

Bookmarks View

Eclipse has a very helpful 'bookmarking' feature to help you quickly navigate to a line in a source file. In any source document, you can add a bookmark and quickly pull up the exact location in the file using the Bookmarks view.

To add a bookmark, open up a source document and click on the line where you want to add the bookmark. Go to the Edit menu and select Add Bookmark... A dialog box will appear prompting you to name the bookmark:

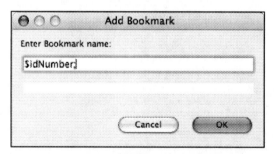

If your cursor was over text, for example, a keyword or variable name, the text will populate in this dialog box by default. However, you can overwrite this with something more descriptive.

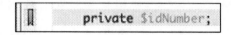

After you click OK, a bookmark icon will appear in the margin of the editor. The bookmark will now appear in the Bookmarks view.

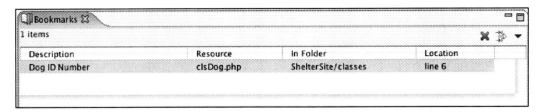

As long as the resource exists in the project, you can double-click on the bookmark at any time to open the file and your cursor will focus on the line of the bookmark. You can also control how the bookmarks are displayed from the toolbar menu.

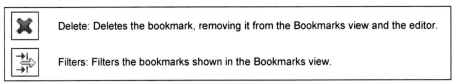

Delete: Deletes the bookmark, removing it from the Bookmarks view and the editor.

Filters: Filters the bookmarks shown in the Bookmarks view.

By default, all bookmarks across all projects are shown. With filters, you can limit the number of bookmarks shown, show bookmarks within a project, within just a resource, within a resource and its children, within a working set that you defined in the Navigator view, or filter bookmarks containing a word pattern.

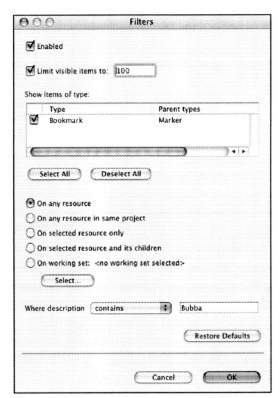

The Bookmark Menu (▽) gives you access to the sorting capabilities of this view and the filters.

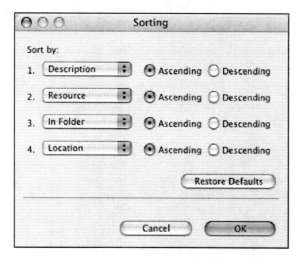

This window allows you to sort your bookmarks on the basis of the various columns in the Bookmarks view. The creation time of the bookmark is captured as metadata when you create the bookmark. The creation time is also a sorting option available in the Sort by: pulldowns.

PHP Browser View

The PHP Browser view is one of the most important features of PHPEclipse. The PHP Browser is a full-fledged web browser operating within Eclipse as a view. It is linked to the editor so any changes you make to a PHP file in the editor will cause the PHP Browser to load or reload the file.

Unlike other IDEs that may simply preview the page without any server-side processing, PHP Browser acts like a real web browser. It will make a request for the page to Apache. If it is a PHP file, Apache will pass the file to the PHP engine for processing before it serves it to PHP Browser. The result is that you will see exactly what your visitors will see. All PHP code is processed and you will not see PHP code outputted to the screen as you do in simple preview functions.

For example, suppose we have a web page that looks like this:

```
<html>
    <head>
        <title>My Simple Page</title>
    </head>
    <body>
        <h1>This is My Simple Page</h1>
        <p>
        <?php
            echo "Simple Math <br />";

            $var1 = 2;
            $var2 = 3;

            echo $var1 . " + " . $var2 . " = " . ($var1 + $var2);
```

```
        ?>
        </p>
        <p>This is the end of the page.</p>
    </body>
</html>
```

This is a simple page with a mix of raw HTML and PHP code that generates text output to the user. As soon as the file is saved, PHP Browser will load the file and present this:

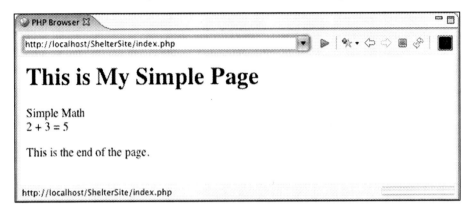

The PHP code is parsed and not simply copied as if the source file is just being displayed. The variables are being manipulated.

Since the PHP Browser is a web browser, the toolbar menu buttons are the same buttons you would find in a typical web browser.

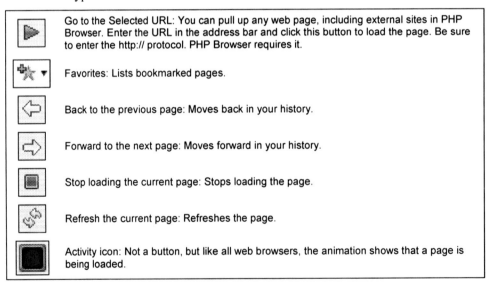

Before we can use the PHP Browser, we will need to make changes to preferences within Eclipse. We will need to know Apache's document root, which we saw in Chapter 2.

Open the appropriate preferences by selecting Window | Preferences | PHPEclipse Web Development | Project Defaults.

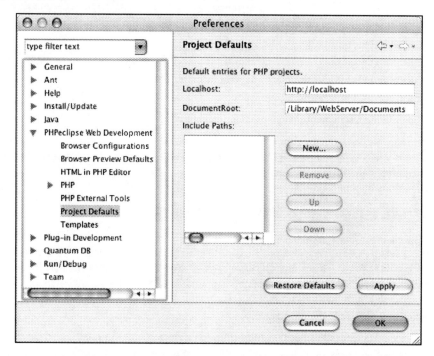

In the Localhost field, type in the URL of your local machine with the http protocol directive. Usually, http://localhost will suffice. If your machine's name server setting has problems with this, try http://127.0.0.1 or http://your_ip_address.

Enter your Apache configuration's document root setting in the DocumentRoot field. This is why we set our initial workspace to exist under the document root directory earlier. For the pages to be served and processed, Apache must have access to them.

If any of your projects are not under the document root directory, Eclipse has an option to move the project. Start by creating a directory under document root with the same name as the project. Right-click the project in the Navigator view and select Move... Browse to this new directory and click OK. Eclipse will automatically move all project files and references to this new location.

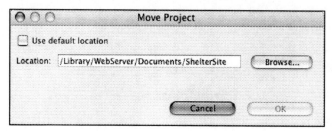

Previously, to show a parsed web page would require the developer to switch out of their development tool, into a web browser with the file loaded, and hit the *Refresh* button. The PHP Browser makes this practice archaic. The PHP Browser will automatically refresh the page when you send a Save command to a PHP script being edited in the editor. You constantly have a PHP-rendered version of the page in front of you.

This view works by using some of the controversial native interfaces of the SWT. The SWT includes a web browser, called the SWT Browser Widget. The Browser Widget itself is what acts as a web browser. The PHP Browser interfaces with this widget. The widget's HTML rendering engine is dependent on your operating system. The widget uses the rendering engine of popular web browsers for a particular operating system—KHTML from the Safari browser for Mac OS X, Gecko from Mozilla browser for Linux, and MSHTML from Internet Explorer for Windows. Note that the widget only uses the HTML rendering engine. It will not have other interpreters or engines such as JavaScript nor ActiveX on Windows.

Personalizing Your Perspectives

Eclipse's architecture is designed to be highly adaptable to your needs. This philosophy carries over to the interface. In the Windows menu, Eclipse offers several ways to change perspectives to suit how you work. These various options allow you to change menu items, toolbar items, and which views are associated with which perspectives, and to create new perspectives.

Customize Perspectives

Your menu options and toolbar icons can be changed in Customize Perspectives. These changes affect the perspective currently being used. They are not universal.

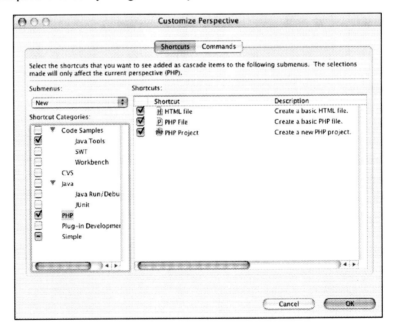

This view allows you to make items available in the File | New menu, the Window | Open Perspective menu, and the Window | Show view menu. You may have noticed that the default setting for those three menus is a bit skimpy. For example, when you create a new document in the PHP perspective, the only shortcut available is PHP File. Similarly, in Open Perspective, the only option available is Other...

To add items to those menus, select the Submenus you want to change. In the Shortcut Categories: window, select a perspective and check the items you would like to include whenever you click on the New menu.

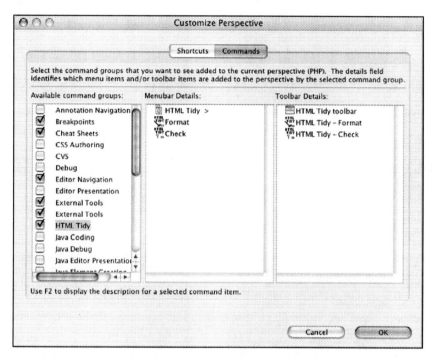

The Commands tab gives you control over which menu bar and toolbar items appear in the perspective. In this tab, Available command groups are listed in the left column. Each command group may have items in the Menubar and Toolbar. These items are listed in the center and right columns.

In this example, in the PHP perspective, if we were to uncheck the HTML Tidy option, all the HTML Tidy buttons would be removed from the toolbars and menu bars. Command groups are created by plug-in developers, therefore we cannot pick and choose which items to include within a group.

Perspective Layouts

In Eclipse, you can customize perspectives to show any view from those available. You also have control over where the views are laid out. To further customize how your Workbench looks, you can resize panes and move views to other panes. Each pane can be resized by hovering your mouse cursor over its border. Your cursor will change to a *resize* cursor, at which point you can move the border like a spreadsheet column.

To move a view into another pane, grab the view's tab and drag it to another pane. If you put it in a pane that already has other views, your view will automatically be stacked with the other views in that pane.

Save Perspective As...

You can create or modify the views that appear by default in a perspective. Open all the views you would like to include and lay them out to your preference.

Give this perspective a name. If you choose a name from an existing perspective, a dialog will prompt you asking if you really want to replace the template. If you select a new name the perspective will appear in all future perspective choices.

Reset Perspective

If you make a mistake, select Reset Perspective to revert the perspective back to its original order.

Close Perspective

This option closes the active perspective.

Close All Perspectives

This option closes all the files and views opened in the Workbench.

Summary

Eclipse uses perspectives to accomplish tasks. A perspective is designed to do one thing—for example, debug an application, view a database. Views are the individual tasks. A perspective uses several groups of views to accomplish its mission. The primary perspective that we will be using for PHP development is the PHP perspective. Among the important views available to us are the Navigator view, which allows us to organize and see our file system, and the PHP Browser, which is a web browser built into Eclipse.

If we are not happy with the way things are laid out in Eclipse, we have several options that allow us to change this. In the Window menu, there are tools that allow us to customize menu items and change which views are used in a perspective.

4
Writing PHP Code with Eclipse

At this point, we have an understanding of Eclipse and how it works. We have a good sense of its features and its Java-centric quirks. We have also set up a development environment based on Apache and PHP. With this, we can now start to create a PHP web application using Eclipse. In this chapter, we will see how to set up a basic application as a project and how to use the editor for code writing. Later, we will walk through creating a whole web application from start to finish. In the process, we will explore how PHPEclipse integrates with other important Eclipse plug-ins and external PHP-related projects.

We will go deeper into our example application of the animal shelter website.

Creating a Project

Each application in Eclipse is organized in a project. All the files needed by the application to run are under the project. In a typical PHP web application, this would include PHP files, HTML templates, images, JavaScript files, and CSS stylesheets.

To create a new project, go to the main menu and click on File | New | Project... This will invoke the New Project wizard.

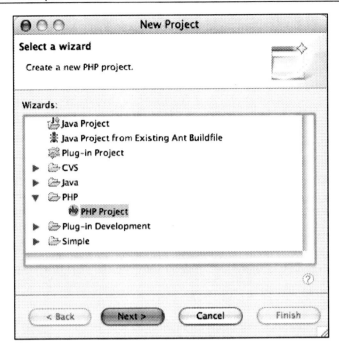

The first screen of this wizard allows you to select the type of application to create. All but one of these application types are available in the standard Eclipse SDK. The lone exception is the PHP Project, which is available courtesy of PHPEclipse. Since we're creating a PHP web application, click on PHP Project and then the Next button.

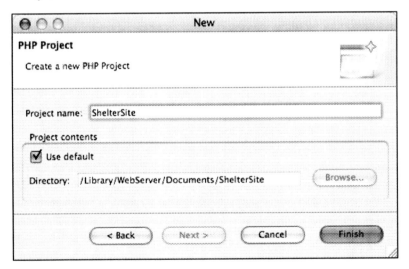

This screen will require us to give a name to the application. The second part asks us if we would like to store the files in the default workspace. If the Use default checkbox is checked, Eclipse will automatically create a directory of the same name under the workspace. If the Use default box is not checked, we can browse to another location to store the files in the file system. This is one of the methods to override the default workspace. Give the application a name and click on the Finish button.

When this is done, your application will be listed in the Navigator view as a project. Underneath the project are the files that belong to the application. Right now, it is empty except for a .project file. This file is used by Eclipse to keep track of projects and their interactions with Eclipse.

Adding Directories

We will add a few subdirectories and source code files to the project in order to build our application.

To create a new directory, select File | New | Folder from the main menu:

In this example, we are creating a subdirectory named classes to store our PHP classes. Click on the name of a project in which you wish to create a subdirectory. In this case, it would be the ShelterSite project. Enter the name of the subdirectory in the Folder name field. We are simply going to call the subdirectory classes. When you click on Finish, this will create a directory under the project workspace in both the file system and Navigator view. If you click on the Advanced button, this will give you access to a powerful file mapping feature of Eclipse. This feature will allow you to bring other areas of your file system into your project.

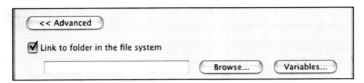

By clicking on the Link to folder in the file system checkbox, you can add a directory that lies outside a project's workspace either by typing in the full path of the directory or browsing with the Browse... button. Further, you can define variable shortcuts to use in this field by clicking on the Variables... button. This will bring up the Select Path Variable window:

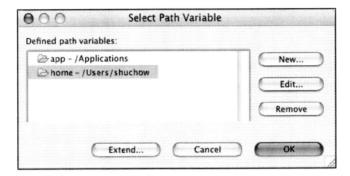

In this example, we have two example variables defined. The app variable will link to this computer's Applications directory and home will link to my home directory. Clicking on New... will bring up a dialog box that asks for two parameters—the name (or shortcut) you wish to assign and the directory that the shortcut maps to. Once you create a mapping name, whenever you type this name in the Folder name field of the New Folder dialog box, it will go directly to this directory. You can use this as a shorthand device for more complicated paths, or it can be used as a mapping to resources that lie outside a project's default workspace.

After you create a directory, it will appear underneath the project in the Navigator view. Here, we have created two other directories under ShelterSite—one for images and one for styles.

Creating PHP Files

As expected for a Java IDE, the standard Eclipse download easily lets you create files geared towards Java development. Templates and wizards to create things like classes, interfaces, and packages are easily accessible. PHPEclipse expands on this and helps you easily create PHP and HTML files.

In this example, we will create a PHP object class for the ShelterSite project. To create a PHP or HTML file, select the directory where you want the file to go in the Navigator view. Go to the File | New | PHP File... option. This will bring up the PHP New File wizard.

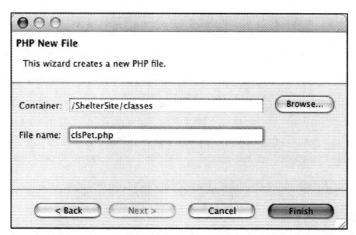

The Container field is the project and subdirectory under which the file will be created. This is the same location as you clicked on at the start. You do not have to modify this field if you selected the right directory in the Navigator view. However, you can use this field to place a file outside of the workspace.

Give the file a name in the File name field. Click on the Finish button and Eclipse will create this file.

You can also create PHP files, as well as other file types, by selecting the File | New | Other... option instead of PHP File... This will bring up the New File wizard.

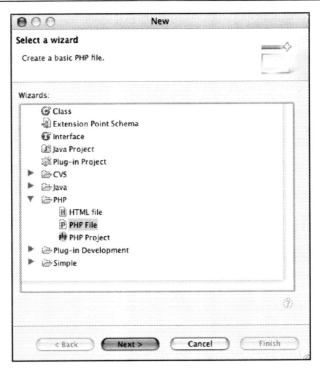

In this wizard, we can select the source file type of any language or project we are working in. Highlight the file type and click on the Next button. The screens thereafter will ask for information specific to the project type or language.

Code Templates

Notice that Eclipse automatically generates a comment block every time you create a PHP file. If you create an HTML file, you'll notice that Eclipse automatically includes standard tags such as <DOCTYPE> and <HTML> in this file. If your company has a standard template for source code files, you can customize these templates to fit your requirements. You can add things like the creation date and your name. PHPEclipse adopts a powerful template feature of the Java IDE to build these code blocks.

To edit these templates, go to Window | Preferences… | PHPEclipse Web Development | PHP | Code Templates in the main menu. This will bring up the code templates Preferences.

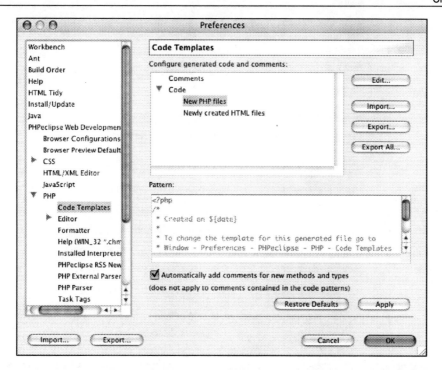

Select the template for the type of file you wish to edit—PHP or HTML. You can preview the template in the Pattern field. Click on the Edit... button to edit the template in the Edit Template dialog box.

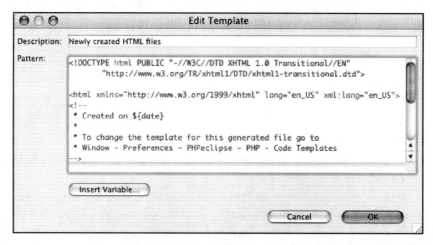

You can manually edit the template from here. A number of auto-insert variables are available in the Insert Variable... button. The code template feature is borrowed from the JDT. Therefore, some variables, like package name, are not relevant for PHP development. However, most variables are useful such as the date and time, to-do tasks, file name, user name, and project name.

Variable	Code	Description
Date	${date}	Date of file creation.
Dollar Sign	$$	Since dollar signs are used to indicate a variable name in the template, to add a dollar sign in a template, use two dollar signs.
File Name	${file_name}	The name of this file.
Package Declaration	${package_declaration}	Not implemented by PHPEclipse.
Package Name	${package_name}	Not implemented by PHPEclipse.
Project Name	${project_name}	Not implemented by PHPEclipse.
Time	${time}	Time of file creation.
Todo	${todo}	Adds a to-do item to the Task view.
Type Declaration	${type_declaration}	Not implemented by PHPEclipse.
Type Name	${type_name}	Not implemented by PHPEclipse.
Type Comment	${typecomment}	Not implemented by PHPEclipse.
User	${user}	The account user name on the local machine.
Year	${year}	Year of file creation.

The JDT code template preferences can be changed by selecting Window | Preferences | Java | Code Style | Code Templates from the main menu. These preferences include many more comment options and allow you to control the code that is automatically created by the JDT.

When you have finished editing your templates, you can share them with co-workers and team members by using the Export... and Export All... buttons in the code template's Preferences. The exported files will be XML files mapped to the PHPEclipse plug-in. These files can be easily exchanged between team members. For example, you can place these files on a network server for new employees to download. On the receiving workstations, use the Import... button to integrate the templates with the local copy of Eclipse. This helps ensure that everyone is using the same standard when coding.

The Editor

We will be doing all of our code writing in the editor, so it will help to be familiar with how the editor works and the feedback it gives us.

On the surface, the Eclipse editor looks and acts like a standard text editor. Once we start coding, we will see many time-saving features. Among these are the visual clues Eclipse conveys. Eclipse relies on syntax coloring and icons to communicate information on our work. We can quickly process information on problems and navigate around source code.

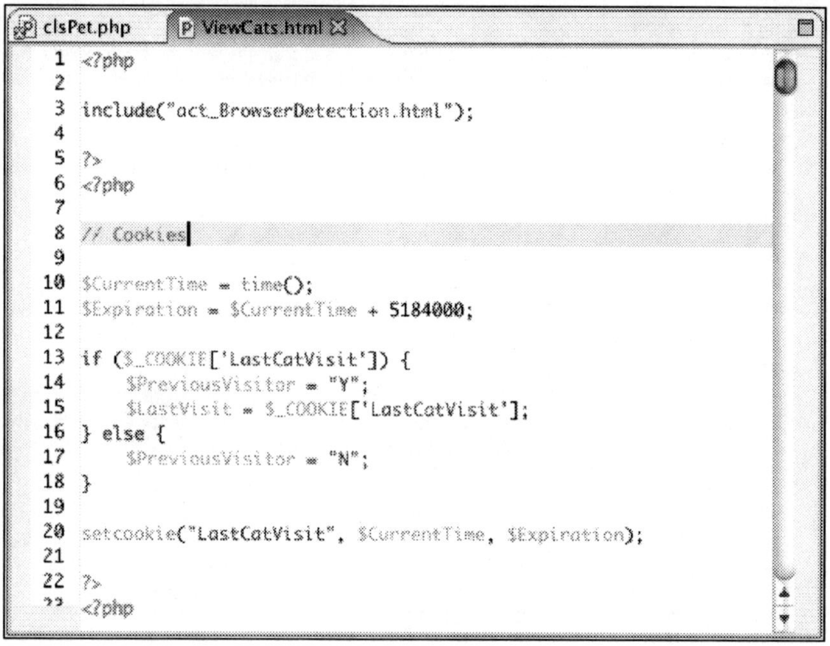

```php
1  <?php
2
3  include("act_BrowserDetection.html");
4
5  ?>
6  <?php
7
8  // Cookies
9
10 $CurrentTime = time();
11 $Expiration = $CurrentTime + 5184000;
12
13 if ($_COOKIE['LastCatVisit']) {
14     $PreviousVisitor = "Y";
15     $LastVisit = $_COOKIE['LastCatVisit'];
16 } else {
17     $PreviousVisitor = "N";
18 }
19
20 setcookie("LastCatVisit", $CurrentTime, $Expiration);
21
22 ?>
23 <?php
```

Editor Visual Aids

As you type, the Eclipse editor marks the syntax of your code with certain colors. When you save, Eclipse reviews your code, marks potential pitfalls, and alerts you via icons in the margin.

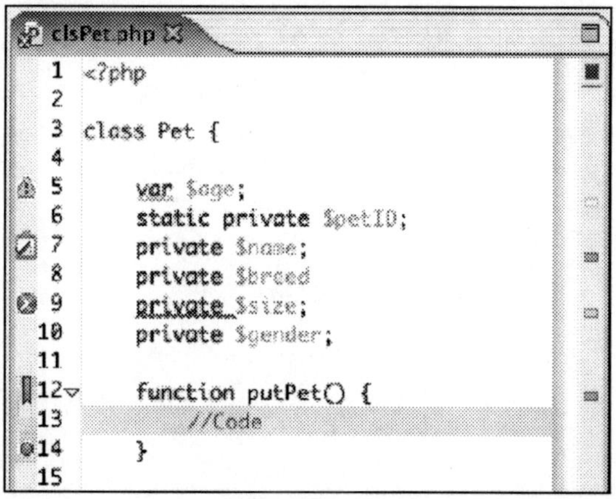

```php
1  <?php
2
3  class Pet {
4
5      var $age;
6      static private $petID;
7      private $name;
8      private $breed;
9      private $size;
10     private $gender;
11
12⌄     function putPet() {
13         //Code
14     }
15
```

The screenshot above shows a typical editor with a few lines of sample code and some problems. Let's first take a look at the left margin.

Line 5: Warning

The keyword `var` is deprecated in PHP 5, but will not cause a runtime error. Syntax problems like this that will not cause the program to fail will be automatically flagged with this warning icon.

Line 7: To-do

This is a note to yourself of something that should be addressed. Eclipse maintains a set of to-do items for you in the Tasks view. To-do items are memos and notes to you within the code. We'll see how to use to-do items later.

Line 9: Error

Errors are problems in the code that will cause the program to fail. In this case, line 8 is missing a semicolon. Eclipse sees the new line at line 9 and tells you that Eclipse was suggesting a semicolon on the previous line. Error icons are automatically added by Eclipse.

Line 12: Bookmark

Bookmarks are placeholders in the code. Chapter 3 covered adding bookmarks from the Edit menu and use of the Bookmarks view. You can also add a bookmark by right-clicking on the margin and selecting **Add Bookmark...** in the contextual menu.

Line 14: Breakpoint

Breakpoints are used to stop code execution during debugging. We will cover debugging in Chapter 5. Breakpoints tell the IDE to give you a snapshot of variable values and program state up to that particular point. To add a breakpoint, right-click on the margin where you want to stop and select **Toggle PHP Breakpoint**.

For any of these left-margin icons, you can hover your mouse cursor over the icon to get the exact message or error that Eclipse is conveying. In the right margin is the overview ruler. The overview ruler shows all of the left-margin icons in the page. The overview ruler is scaled to the entire page so that you will always see all of the issues on a page in the overview ruler. Clicking on any of these rectangles in the right margin will take you to the exact line with the marker. All of the items in the overview ruler are also represented in an appropriate view. For example, bookmarks in the overview ruler also have a corresponding item in the Bookmarks view, and problems will be listed in the Problems view.

At the top of the editor, each open file is represented by a tab. The tab will have the same icon for the file as in the Navigator view and this icon depends on the file type and the name of the file. The tab may have other symbols on it depending on the state of the file. An asterisk is a visual notice that the file has been changed, but not saved:

As in the left margin in the editor, the yellow caution icon tells you that there is a non-fatal error in the code:

Again, as in the left margin in the editor, the red error icon tells you that there is a fatal error in the code of this page. Fatal error icons take precedence over warning icons. A page with a fatal error icon may also have a warning in the code.

A tab with just the icon and name tells you that there is nothing wrong with the code:

Customizing the Editor

PHPEclipse's editor can be customized to your own work style in its own set of preferences. These preferences are located in the Window | Preferences... | PHPEclipse Web Development | PHP menu option.

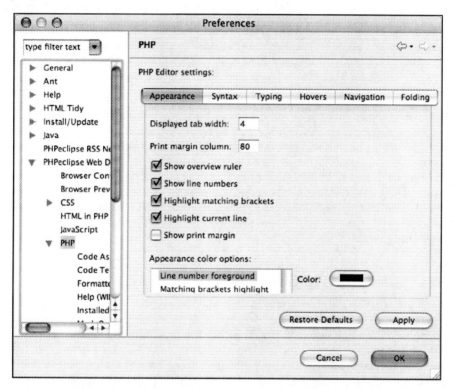

The Appearance tab controls most of the editor's higher-level behaviors. The overview ruler can be turned on and off here. You will probably want to turn on line numbers as soon as you get started with Eclipse as this feature is turned off by default. Check the Show line numbers checkbox in this tab and line numbers will appear in the left margin of the editor. Other editor behaviors that you can toggle include highlighting the matching curly bracket when your cursor is next to a curly bracket, highlighting the current line you are on, and showing the print margin of a page of code. You can change the color of all of these highlighting options in the Appearance color options section of this tab.

In the Syntax tab, you can change the colors that the editor uses to differentiate keywords and sections of code. For example, you'll notice that the class and return keywords are maroon in the editor. In the Syntax tab, you can give these keywords different colors.

As you type code in the editor, you'll notice that it does helpful things such as automatically closing parentheses, quotes, and curly brackets when you open them. These real-time typing aides can be turned on and off in the Typing tab.

With any of the margin icons that we saw previously, you can hover the mouse cursor over them to get more information. Warnings and error icons will give the specific reason for which the error occurred. The Hover tab affects this action. Although there are options on this tab for more than one type of hover, PHPEclipse keeps the Combined Hover option clicked and activated. Combined Hover will turn on all hovers automatically. Although the option to turn off Combined Hover and individually control all other hovers exists, Eclipse will not remember changes to this setting.

The Navigation tab has only one option, Support hyperlink style navigation for "Open Declaration". This option turns files and directories that are referenced in code into hyperlinks much like in web pages. Hovering over the file or directory in the code will underline the item. Clicking on the name of the file will cause Eclipse to open up that resource in the editor. These files and directories may be parameters passed in `include()` functions or regular hyperlinks in anchor tags.

The Folding tab controls folding of function blocks. If this box is checked, you'll notice a small circle icon with either a plus (+) or a minus sign (-) inside, next to comment block, function declaration, and class declaration blocks of code. A plus sign indicates that the whole block is shown in the editor. A minus sign indicates that the block is hidden except for the first line of the block. Clicking on this circle will toggle the block's collapsed and expanded state. This lets you hide comment blocks, functions and classes that are finished. This keeps the editor clean as you work. Note that Eclipse will not remember the state of which blocks are collapsed and expanded. By default, when you open a saved file, comment blocks are collapsed while function and class declarations are expanded.

Creating a Web Application

At this point, we know the basics of using Eclipse for PHP development. We have seen the project-oriented nature of Eclipse and how projects relate to the file system. We have also briefly looked at the editor. We have been introduced to the various icons and symbols used in the Eclipse editor and we have walked through customizing the editor using the Preferences option. There are many other features of the editor. Let's walk through creating a whole web application to see the process in its entirety and how to use features in an actual development context.

In this example, we will create a simple application to pull a list of adoptable animals from a database. This application will be a simple object-oriented PHP web application. We will use concepts such as inheritance to demonstrate features of PHPEclipse. We will create all the files and lines of code necessary for this application. However, the complete application is also available for download at `http://www.packtpub.com/support/book/phpeclipse`.

Setting Up the Database

The very first thing we will need to do is to create a database to store pet information. This database will need to work with the code examples in this chapter. The quickest way to do this is to download the source files for this application and import the file named `shelter.sql` into your MySQL instance.

`shelter.sql` is an SQL data dump file. It creates the database and table schema, and populates some sample data using standard SQL. This file uses CREATE statements to make the database and the tables. This is not a permission usually granted to non-administrators. If you followed the instructions in Chapter 2, you can use the root account on your local version of MySQL to import this file. If you are using a remote database that you do not have root access to, you will need the help of your database administrator to import this file

If you are using a MySQL GUI front-end program such as phpMyAdmin, you can use the entire `shelter.sql` file as an import script. You can also import this file from the command line if you do not have a front-end program.

> If you are using phpMyAdmin, you will need to allow Drop Database statements in your `config.inc.php` file before you can import `shelter.sql`. To do this, open `config.inc.php` and set the `$cfg['AllowUserDropDatabase']` variable to `true`.

Make sure that the MySQL server is running and type this into the command line, where */path/to* is your file system path to the MySQL executable and the `shelter.sql` file:

```
Buttercup:~ shuchow$ /path/to/mysql -u root -p < /path/to/shelter.sql
```

This command will execute the `shelter.sql` statements into MySQL. Notice the `-u root -p` portion. This tells the command line MySQL client to log in as root. You will be prompted for the root password. If you are not using MySQL, or if you are have trouble importing `shelter.sql`, you can create the database and tables manually. Here is the schema that you will need to create in your database:

DATABASE NAME: Shelter

TABLE: tCat

Field Name	Type	Null?	Key	Default	Extras
CatID	INT(11)	No	Primary	NULL	Auto Increment
Name	VARCHAR(40)	No			
Gender	CHAR(1)	No			
Age	INT(3)	No			
Breed	VARCHAR(100)	No			

After you create the database, insert some sample data in tCat. Be sure that a user has at least *SELECT* rights to this database.

> This user will be used by the web application to access the data. You'll need this user regardless of whether you're using MySQL or another database.

Setting Up the Project

Using what we have learned earlier in this chapter, we will now use Eclipse to create the project and directory structure for our application.

We have already created a project named 'ShelterSite' project and subdirectories under it; if you haven't followed those steps then create a new project by going to the File | New | Project... option. Create a new PHP Project. Give this project the name 'ShelterSite'.

Attach the workspace to a directory under your Apache installation's document root. We already had to specify a default workspace when we first started Eclipse. If you followed the Eclipse startup directions in Chapter 3, the default workspace should already be your document root.

In the Navigator view, create two directories, one named classes and the other styles. Do this by clicking on the ShelterSite project and selecting the File | New | Folder option for each directory.

Creating the Objects

We will need four objects for our application:

- A Database object to handle connections
- A Cat object to handle cats in our system
- A CatView object to handle objects required to view cat details
- A Pet object that will act as the parent class to Cat

Create four empty PHP files in the classes directory. To do this, click on classes in the Navigator view and then select the option File | New | PHP File.

Give them the following names:

- clsDatabase.php
- clsCat.php
- clsCatView.php
- clsPet.php

Creating the View Files

Now let's create a few front-end, display pages. We'll create a PHP page that visitors will request to view the list of animals in the shelter. To make the page presentable, we'll create a cascading stylesheet to format the page.

Create an empty PHP file under the top level of the application named viewCats.php. Do this by clicking once on the ShelterSite project and going to File | New | PHP File menu option.

Create an empty stylesheet in the `styles` directory. Do this by clicking once on the styles directory and going to the File | New | File menu option. Name the file `shelter.css`.

Your Navigator view should now look like this:

Writing the Database Class

We're finally ready to start writing PHP code. Let's begin with the 'Database class'. When instantiated, this class will create a database connection, and store that connection in a class member variable. We can take this connection and pass it around to other functions that interact with the database.

> In the examples in this book, we will be using the new object features of PHP 5. These new features include visibility limiters (public/private) for functions and class member variables. This code will only work with PHP 5. The latest versions of XAMPP and Entropy's packages have PHP 5 available. If you are using PHP 4, the sample code at `http://www.packtpub.com/support/book/phpeclipse` includes a version of this application written for PHP 4. The code will look different, but the PHPEclipse features and object-oriented principles will work the same. For more information on the new features of PHP 5, see the appendix in the PHP manual at `http://www.php.net/manual/en/migration5.php`.

Open the `clsDatabase.php` file by double-clicking on it in the Navigator view. We'll begin by declaring the class member variable, `$dbConn`, that will hold the database connection. However, we're going to deliberately make a spelling mistake.

```
<?php
    class Database
    {
        privte $dbConn;
```

Notice that the keyword `private` is misspelled. In the editor, this misspelling will be underlined in red. Here we see one advantage of the IDE in action. The editor knows that in PHP, `privte` should not be there. It has two clues to work with.

First, this line is immediately after a class declaration. Second, it's immediately followed by a variable name. Therefore, this must be a class member variable declaration. The editor knows that the class member variable declarations begin with one of the keywords public, private, or package, and privte does not fit. Hence, this must be an error and should be flagged.

If you save the file at this point, PHPEclipse knows that this will cause a runtime error and will warn you by placing an error icon in the margin. When files are saved, the editor goes through the source code and looks for errors. This means that the left-margin icon will not appear exactly at the moment an error is created, nor will fixed errors make the icon disappear until after you save your changes.

In this case, it should be clear to you that the error is a misspelling. However, there may be some errors that are not so clear. There may be occasions where you and Eclipse disagree on whether there is an error. Some code may appear fine to you, while Eclipse marks it as a problem. When this happens, you can hover your mouse cursor over the red underline of the error or the error margin on the left. After a few seconds, the editor will pop up a message describing what is wrong and the error will appear in the Problems view. This will give you the reason why Eclipse believes there is a problem.

```
1   <?php
2
3   class Database
4   {
5
6       privte $dbConn;
7       Parser error "'public' 'private' or 'protected' modifier expected for field declarations."
8
9
```

Fix this spelling error and begin to create our first function. This function will be a public function to get the $dbConn variable. However, do not completely type the keyword 'function'. Only type the 'func' part. Your code should look like this:

```
<?php
    class Database
    {
        private $dbConn;
        public func
```

As you type, the code assist help system may pop up automatically. It may not automatically pop up depending on your hardware specs, preference settings, and whether you are typing a new line or editing an existing line. If it does not, you can always invoke the system manually. With the I-beam cursor remaining after the 'c', hit *Ctrl+Space* to launch the code assist help system:

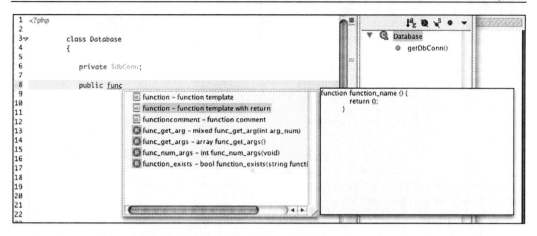

The code assist system evaluates what you are doing at the moment, and gives you a list of possible things that are allowed at that point. In other words, it is a context-sensitive hint system.

Right now, the system knows that func has already been typed. Therefore, we are trying to either type the keyword function, or we are trying to type in one of the built-in PHP functions that begin with func. The former are code templates—initially populated by PHPeclipse—editable in the preferences, and the latter are built directly into PHPeclipse. Refer to the screenshot shown below; templates have the name and a short description on the left window. The right window has the actual template. In the built-in function list, we see the function name and method signature. The right window will give us a description of what the function does.

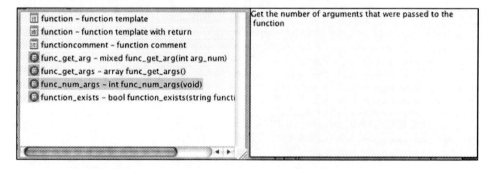

Right now, we are creating a function that will return the database connection object to the caller. The function template with return is what we need, so select it by either scrolling down with the arrow keys and hitting *Enter*, or double-clicking on it with your mouse. PHPeclipse takes the stored template and drops it where your cursor is. Notice that function_name is enclosed in a blue rectangle. This is because it is defined as a variable in the template. It currently has the cursor focus. If you begin typing, your text will appear in place of function_name.

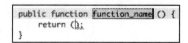

We're creating a getter method for the dbConn class member variable, so name this function getDbConn. Make it return the dbConn variable. Your code at this point should look like this:

```php
<?php
    class Database
    {
        private $dbConn;
        public function getDbConn()
        {
            return $this->dbConn;
        }
}
```

Let's see how the templating system works by creating our own template. PHPEclipse currently does not have a template for PHP 5-style constructors. We'll create one and use it in our project. Templates are defined in the menu option Windows | Preferences... | PHPEclipse Web Development | PHP | Templates.

This will bring up the template Preferences window. You can see the templates already defined. PHPEclipse creates default templates for PHP keywords, HTML tags, and PHPDoc tags. Here, you can control all your templates. PHPEclipse also includes the ability to share your templates with project team members with an Import.../Export... function.

> PHPEclipse remembers the default templates, so if you make a mistake and need to revert or restore a deleted template, you can do that by clicking the Restore Defaults button.

We're going to create a new template, so click on this window's New... button.

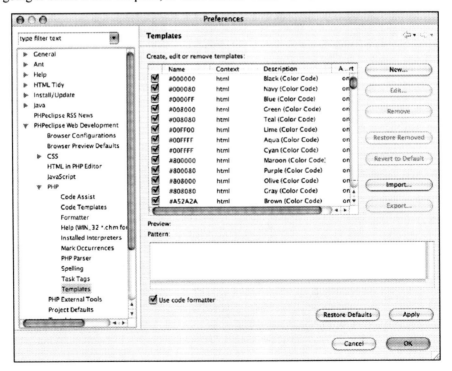

This will bring up a New Template dialog box. The Name field is important because the editor matches what we have begun to type with the names of templates to make suggestions in the code assist box. After we're done, this 'public constructor' will appear when we type pub in the editor and invoke code assist. The Description is what will show up next to the Name in code assist. The Pattern box is the actual chunk of code that will be the template.

Fill this dialog box with the values shown in the following image:

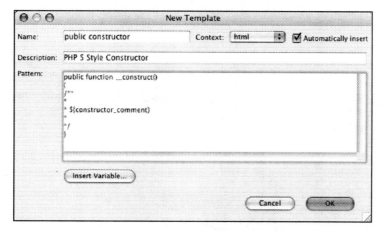

In template editing mode, dollar signs designate a variable. When you reach the dollar sign, Eclipse will show you a list of auto-fill variables. You can select one of these to automatically populate the function. For example, using the date variable, you can automatically add a template that inserts the current date whenever the template is invoked.

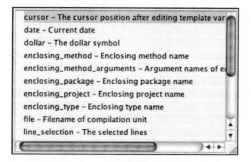

We are not going to use any of the available variables suggested. Instead, we're going to create a new, custom variable named constructor_comment. This will allow us to fill in the value at a later time.

Click the OK button and you'll return to the Templates preference window. Note that our public constructor is now on the list of templates. Click on the OK button to close the Templates preferences window.

Back in the editor, type pu and then invoke code assist by pressing *Ctrl+Space*:

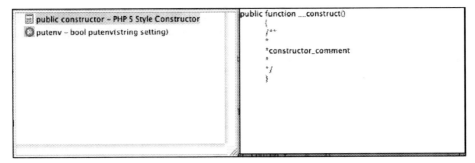

We now have two options in code assist—our template and putenv(), the only native PHP function that begins with pu. When our template is selected, the right window shows the code that we entered for this template:

The custom variable name, constructor_comment, will have the cursor's focus, so just begin typing to enter the variable value. Type in:

```
Constructor instantiates db connection
```

This will populate the comment block. The rest of the constructor will connect to the MySQL server and select our database. Here is the rest of the Database class:

```php
<?php
    class Database
    {
        private $dbConn;
        public function getDbConn()
        {
            return $this->dbConn;
        }
        public function __construct()
        {
/**
*
*Constructor instantiates db connection
*
*/
            $this->dbConn = @mysql_connect("localhost", "eclipse",
"melanie") or die("Couldn't connect to the MySQL server.");
            mysql_select_db("Shelter", $this->dbConn) or die("Couldn't connect
to the Shelter database.");
        }
    }
?>
```

Note that my call to `mysql_connect` passes the user as `eclipse` with a password of `melanie`. Replace this with your user's name and password.

Writing the Pet Class

The `Pet` class is used as a parent class. Our `Cat` class will inherit from `Pet`. If we had a `Dog` or `Iguana` class, it would also inherit from `Pet`. In our example, our database stores the age of a pet in months. We will add a function in `Pet` to translate months into years and months and output this into a string.

Open the `clsPet.php` file and enter this code into the page:

```php
<?php

class Pet
{
    public function translateMonths($months)
    {
        $returnMe = false;

        if ($months < 0 || !is_numeric($months))
        {
        }
        else if ($months < 12)
        {
            $returnMe = "0 years, " . $months . " months";
        }
        else
        {
            $years = floor($months / 12);
            $months = $months % 12;
            $returnMe = $years . " years, " . $months . " months";
        }

        return $returnMe;
    }
    public function __construct()
    {
    }
}
?>
```

In case you are not familiar with the `floor()` function, this would be a good time to demonstrate the help features of PHPEclipse.

Eclipse's plug-in architecture extends into the help system. Plug-in developers can create end-user documentation for their plug-ins and integrate it into Eclipse's main help functionality. Normally, the main help system is invoked by selecting the menu option Help | Help Contents.

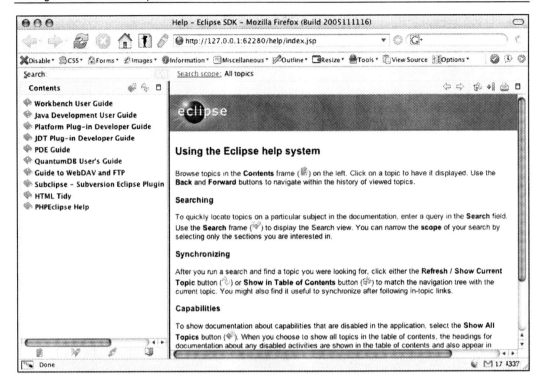

The normal Eclipse SDK download includes help topics on the Eclipse environment and JDT. Plug-in developers add topics for their own plug-ins. Users can browse the topics, search through a topic, or search through all topics for a term.

PHPEclipse contributes to the help system by adding documentation for HTML Tidy, QuantumDB, and the official PHP documentation (http://www.php.net/manual/en/). PHPEclipse extends the Eclipse help files by integrating the PHP documentation into the editor. Suppose you want to look up what the floor() function does. In the editor, highlight the entire function. Right-click on the highlighted function and select PHP Help from the contextual menu. This will launch the Eclipse help system and open up the function's definition from the official PHP documentation.

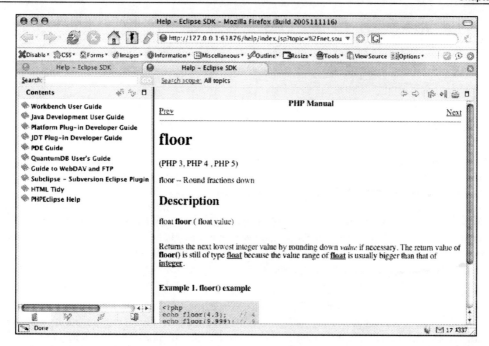

The whole PHP reference guide is available to you wherever you go because the help system files are stored locally on the machine where PHPEclipse is installed. An internet connection is not required. This is especially helpful to laptop users.

Writing the Cat Class

We'll now write the class that will represent an individual cat. Open up clsCat.php and type in the following code block:

```php
<?php

require_once("clsPet.php");

class Cat extends Pet
{
    private $catID;
    private $name;
    private $gender;
    private $age;
    private $breed;

    public function setCatID($catID) { $this->catID = $catID; }
    public function getCatID() { return $this->catID; }

    public function setName($name) { $this->name = $name; }
    public function getName() { return $this->name; }

    public function setGender($gender) { $this->gender = $gender; }
    public function getGender() { return $this->gender; }
```

```php
    public function setAge($age) { $this->age = $age; }
    public function getAge() { return $this->age; }

    public function setBreed($breed) { $this->breed = $breed; }
    public function getBreed() { return $this->breed; }

    public function __construct() { }

  }
?>
```

There are a couple of things to try as you type this.

First, is the ability of Eclipse to open any project files referenced in code. The Cat class is a subclass of Pet, so we need to include the file with the Pet class. To open the Pet class from here, highlight clsPet.php, right-click on it, and select Open Declaration/Include. If clsPet.php is not open, Eclipse will open it and the editor will bring that page forward. Otherwise, Eclipse will switch you to that page. If you selected Support hyperlink style navigation for "Open Declaration" in the PHP editor preferences, clsPet.php will be underlined and become a link when you hover your mouse cursor over it. Simply click on the link to open clsPet.php. Note that targeted the file must be in the project. Open Declaration/Include will not work for any files that are not in the project, including those that reside in the includes directives of the php.ini file and any external PEAR files.

Second, we can play with the Outline view in action. After you have written the entire class, notice how the Outline view gives you a high-level view of your class. In this example, we see the import declarations of this class, the class member variables, and the methods we have defined.

Double-clicking on any of these items will take us to the line number where they are declared. In the JDT, the Outline view is updated in real time as you type. However, in PHPEclipse, you may have to toggle the Outline view options to get the view to refresh. Also, when the file is initially opened, the Outline view will be current.

Writing the View Class

Our final class is a viewer class that is instantiated by the PHP page that the visitor calls, clsCatview.php. The methods in this class will not control display. This job is reserved for template pages and stylesheets. Instead, it will provide all the data that is needed by template pages.

In our example, we only need one method. This method will retrieve all the cats from the database, put them all in a cat object, put all the cat objects into an array, and return the array to the caller.

```php
<?php

class CatView
{
    public function getAllCatsArray($conn)
    {
        require_once("clsCat.php");

        $sql = "SELECT * FROM tCat ORDER BY CatID";
        $e = mysql_query($sql, $conn);
        $catArr = array();
        $i = 0;

        while ($rs = mysql_fetch_array($e))
        {
            $catArr[$i] = new Cat();
            $catArr[$i]->setCatID($rs['CatID']);
            $catArr[$i]->setName($rs['Name']);
            $catArr[$i]->setGender($rs['Gender']);
            $catArr[$i]->setAge($rs['Age']);
            $catArr[$i]->setBreed($rs['Breed']);
            $i++;
        }

        return $catArr;
    }
}
?>
```

When you are calling the setter methods in the while loop, try invoking code assist. Now that we've created a few classes with class member variables and methods, you'll notice that code assist is aware of them. On top of the PHP functions, keywords, and templates, code assist also knows what else is going on in the project.

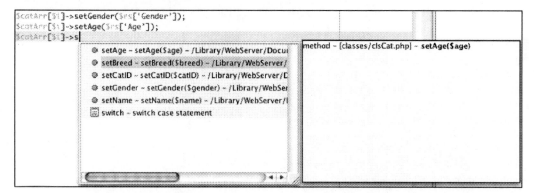

If you've used code assist in the JDT, you'll know that it is smart enough not to include variables and methods if the scope does not allow them; for example, private variables of another class. PHPEclipse's code assist is not yet smart enough to recognize visibility modifiers in PHP classes. However, the PHP interpreter will catch these mistakes at run time.

Since PHPEclipse knows that a class in your application has a certain method, you can also open the file that defines the method from the editor. You no longer have to invoke a search of files to find which file defines the setAge() method. This is also invoked through the Open Declaration/ Include functionality. Try this by highlighting setAge() or any of the other calls to setter methods in this class. Right-click on the method name and select Open Declaration/Include. clsCat.php should open and the editor will take you to the line where the setAge() method is defined with the method name already highlighted.

We can do a manual search of files for the string setAge to demonstrate Eclipse's find and search features.

The difference between 'find' and 'search' in Eclipse is scope. Find, invoked by going to Edit | Find/Replace…, finds a string in the page that is opened in the editor. Eclipse's replace function is also invoked in this screen. This Find/Replace feature works much like a standard word processor's find and replace. The key difference is the ability to search for a regular expression and the ability to limit your search within a page by highlighting a block of lines before invoking the Find/Replace window.

Search is invoked by going to Search | Search…

Search works very much like Find/Replace, except Search can find strings across the workspace, project, or any defined working sets. You can add even more precision in the files to search by limiting the files searched to file names with a certain string pattern.

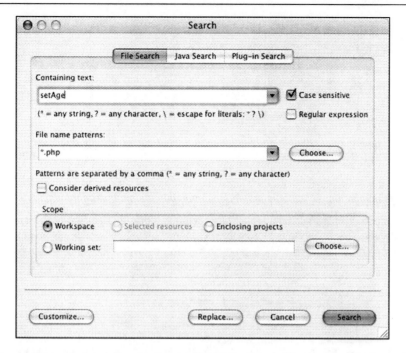

If you wish to replace a string using the Search function, first define the scope and search pattern in the Search window. Then, click on Replace... The search will execute and Eclipse will bring up the Replace window:

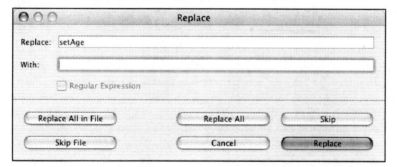

Eclipse will attempt to replace the strings by going through each file found during the search. You can choose to skip a file, skip the instance in the file, replace all in a file, or replace all instances everywhere.

The search results will appear in the Search view.

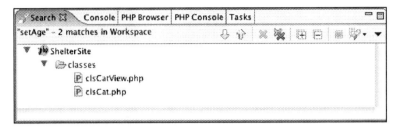

Here we see the results for our search for setAge. It is found in two files. Double-clicking on either file will launch the file and the cursor will jump to the line with the search pattern.

Eclipse has very powerful and useful post-search features, too. In the Search view's toolbar, you can click the up and down arrows to scroll through the result set, with each one opening in the editor. You can remove all or one file from the result set, expand or collapse the result trees, cancel a search that is taking too long, or pull up a history of previous searches and their results.

Eclipse Web Tools Platform Project

We now have data objects in our application. They interact with the database and use each other. It's time to write a page to present this data to the user. It would be helpful if our editor knew presentation languages like HTML and CSS. For example, if the editor knew XHTML or CSS, it could warn us if we use a tag or attribute incorrectly. It could also show a hierarchy of our file structure in the Outline view. In other words, it would be very beneficial if we had the same editor tools for HTML and CSS as we have for Java and PHP. Java and PHP get their editing tools from the Java JDT plug-in and PHPEclipse plug-in, respectively. To get similar tools for HTML and CSS, we'll need to turn to other plug-ins. This is where the Eclipse **Web Tools Platform (WTP)** project comes in.

The Eclipse Web Tools Platform is a collection of plug-ins to extend the Eclipse platform for web development. Thanks to the JDT, Eclipse knows Java out of the box. However, it does not know anything about web technologies such as HTML, CSS, and JavaScript. As the demand for web applications—specifically J2EE web applications—grew alongside the popularity of Eclipse, it was evident that Eclipse could and should be a great tool for web application development. The Eclipse WTP project was formed in 2004 and a year later, the first deliverable, version 0.7 of the WTP was released.

The WTP includes source code editors for HTML, JavaScript, CSS, JSP, SQL, XML, DTD, XSD, and WSDL. The main features include each editor's awareness of its respective language, syntax styles (to highlight using colors), and code templates for each language. Also, the plug-in links the editor to the Outline view. The Outline view will report all element tags in the editor and display them in a hierarchal and friendly format.

If you have used PHPEclipse in the past, you will remember the HTML and CSS editor plug-ins bundled with PHPEclipse. As of version 1.1.8, these are no longer included with PHPEclipse. The developers wisely decided to unbundle these plug-ins and leverage the WTP instead. This frees up the PHPEclipse project team from maintaining the editors and allows them to concentrate on making the best Eclipse tool for pure PHP development.

Installing the Web Tools Platform

You can grab the latest version at `http://download.eclipse.org/webtools/downloads/`. Click on the 'Build Name' for the latest Released version. On the Requirements section of the page, you will see the required libraries for the WTP. As of this writing, the WTP requires:

- The WTP itself
- The EMF drive
- The GEF driver
- Java EMF Model Runtime

How you download and install will differ as per your platform.

Installing on Linux and Windows

On the download page, the Eclipse Foundation provides an all-in-one package that includes all three prerequisites as well as the WTP, and the Eclipse SDK itself. Simply download this package and decompress it. The package contains a `plugins` directory and a `features` directory. Installation of this is just like installing PHPEclipse. Move the contents of this `features` directory into the `features` directory underneath the Eclipse installation directory. Move the contents of the `plugins` directory into the `plugins` directory underneath the Eclipse installation directory. Since the all-in-one package includes the Eclipse SDK plug-ins, you will receive messages warning you that some files already exist. It would be wise to not replace those files. Tell the operating system to skip over existing files. Exit and restart Eclipse to load the WTP plug-ins.

Installing on Macintosh

Unfortunately, there is no all-in-one package for the prerequisites and WTP for Mac OS X. But, we can download and decompress all of the prerequisites and install them manually. In the Requirements section of the WTP download page, a direct link to each prerequisite is included. Download each one and decompress it on your hard drive. After expanding, each prerequisite will have a `plugins` and `features` directory. As for Windows/Linux and PHPEclipse installation, transfer their contents into the respective Eclipse installation directories. Finally, download the WTP itself by going to the section titled WebTools Platform; Runtime on the WTP download page. In here, you will also see the `plugins` and `features` directory. Place the contents of these directories underneath their respective directories in the Eclipse installation directory. Exit and restart Eclipse to load the WTP plug-ins.

Writing the View Page

Now we are ready to create the view page. Open the ViewCats.php page and enter this code:

```php
<?php

   require("classes/clsDatabase.php");
   require("classes/clsCatView.php");

   $dbObj = new Database();
   $listingObj = new CatView();

   $listingArr = $listingObj->getAllCatsArray($dbObj->getDbConn());

?>
<!DOCTYPE html PUBLIC "-//W3C//DTD XHTML 1.0 Transitional//EN"
"http://www.w3.org/TR/xhtml1/DTD/xhtml1-transitional.dtd">
<html xmlns="http://www.w3.org/1999/xhtml" lang="en_US" xml:lang="en_US">
  <head>
    <title>Available Cats</title>
    <link href="styles/shelter.css" type="text/css" rel="stylesheet" />
  </head>
  <body>
    <h1>Available Cats</h1>
    <table>
    <tr>
    <th>Name</th>
    <th>ID Number</th>
    <th>Age</th>
    <th>Gender</th>
    <th>Breed</th>
    </tr>
    <?php
       foreach ($listingArr as $key=>$value)
       {
    ?>
    <tr>
    <td><?= $value->getName() ?></td>
    <td><?= $value->getCatID() ?></td>
    <td><?= $value->translateMonths($value->getAge()) ?></td>
    <td><?= $value->getGender() ?></td>
    <td><?= $value->getBreed() ?></td>
    </tr>
    <?
       }
    ?>
    </table>
  </body>
</html>
```

When the file is saved, assuming there are no errors anywhere in the code, the PHP Browser view will be activated. If Apache is running, the page will appear in the PHP Browser view just as a visitor would see it. If there are any errors in your code and PHP is configured to display errors, they would also appear here.

Taking Advantage of the WTP HTML Editor

Unfortunately, if we name our view pages with a `.php` extension, we will not be able to use and see the excellent HTML editor that WTP brings. This is because Eclipse associates extensions with editors, and the `.php` extension is hard-linked to the PHP editor by PHPEclipse. One way to get around this is to tell Apache to treat all HTML files as PHP files. This will give us the ability to have `<?php ?>` tags in `.html` files that can actually execute PHP code. It also gives us a little security through obscurity by not exposing to the world that we have `.php` extensions, and thus are running PHP. In order to do this, add `.html` (and also `.htm` if desired) to this line in your Apache `httpd.conf` file:

```
AddType application/x-httpd-php .php .html .htm
```

The downside to this is that every HTML gets passed to the PHP parser, even if there is no PHP code in the file. Also, your production server may not have this directive set. Double-check with your server's administrator before changing this on your local development workstation. If this can or is being done on the production server, be sure to rename all of your view files to `.html` files to associate the editing with the HTML editor.

If either Apache or MySQL is not running, you can configure Eclipse to send start, stop, and restart messages to the server. Enter the path to your Apache and MySQL binaries in Windows | Preferences... | PHPEclipse Web Development | PHP External Tools. After this screen is configured, you can control Apache and MySQL through the PHP/Apache menu or the Apache and MySQL buttons that appear on the Eclipse toolbar. Note that this feature only works under Windows since *only* the Windows binary can be started, stopped, and restarted with a parameter.

Assuming that Apache is running and everything is configured correctly, this is what you should see in the PHP Browser view: *http:// localhost/Shelter//viewCats.php*

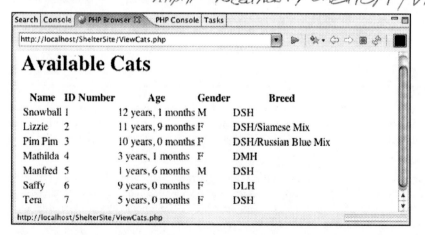

This shows us that our PHP code is working, but from a display standpoint, it is less than optimal. We will use Eclipse's WTP to help us edit the stylesheet.

Open the `shelter.css` stylesheet in the `styles` directory. You can now do this either by double-clicking `shelter.css` in the Navigator view or using the Open Declaration feature in `ViewCats.php`.

In plug-in development, editors inherit a lot of the same features from the main SDK editor. You will notice similar traits between the PHP, Java, HTML, and CSS editors. All the editors use a similar code syntax engine for color syntax customization and template system to create new templates for new files. Since the CSS and HTML editors come from the same development team, you will see even more similarities in features and customization options between the two. You can control the WTP editor preferences in the Windows | Preferences... | Web and XML menu option. From here you can either go to CSS Files | CSS Source or HTML Files | HTML Source menu option. The screen here shows the CSS source Preferences:

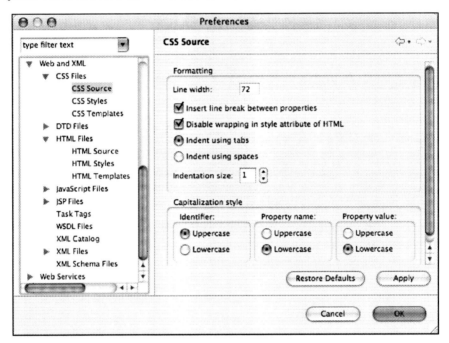

For both, you can edit the metadata behavior of the file. You can choose line-break formats and file encoding at the top-level screen of each editor. Language grammar-specific behavior can be edited in the CSS Source screen. The CSS Styles screen allow you to edit the color syntax of the elements. Finally, CSS Templates allow you to create new file templates.

Back in `shelter.css`, we can begin editing our stylesheet. We will just create a simple stylesheet to modify the font properties in the table cells. As you type an element, be aware that code assist is also available to you. The CSS editor will present possible CSS elements as you type your stylesheet.

```
h1 {
    font-family: Helvetica, Arial, Verdana, san-serif;
    font-size: 24px;
    color: red;
    }
```

```
th {
    font-family: Helvetica, Arial, Verdana, san-serif;
    font-size: 12px;
    font-weight: bold;
    text-align: center;
    padding-right: 15px;
    padding-left: 15px;
}

td {
    font-family: Times, Georgia, serif;
    font-size: 12px;
    text-align: center;
}
```

After you save the shelter.css file, go back to ViewCats.php and click on the refresh button in the PHP Browser view. This page should now look a little more presentable for our audience.

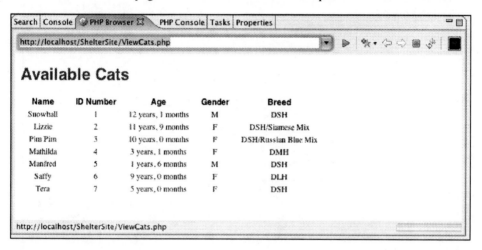

We now have an almost complete PHP web application built in Eclipse. We still have some house-cleaning activities where Eclipse can help us finish.

HTML Cleanup Using HTML Tidy

HTML Tidy is a program that cleans up HTML code and makes sure it is in compliance with W3C standards. Running HTML Tidy on web pages will ensure that your page is error free and renders correctly in browsers.

HTML Tidy itself is an open source project that maintains a library of official HTML tags directly based on the W3C HTML standards. The main product is TidyLib, the libraries, but the project also maintains several front-end programs for TidyLib. The project home page is at http://tidy.sourceforge.net/. Another open source project, Eclipse Tidy integrates TidyLib within Eclipse as a plug-in.

Eclipse Tidy comes bundled with PHPEclipse. Like the CSS and HTML editors, there are plans to have Eclipse Tidy removed from the official PHPEclipse releases. Still, Eclipse Tidy is a great tool that is very useful for web development. Eclipse Tidy makes it very easy to check our code for syntax errors and standards compliance. We will download and install Eclipse Tidy and walk through a code-checking session.

Eclipse Tidy can be downloaded from the SourgeForge site at http://eclipsetidy.sourceforge.net/. As of this writing, the latest version is version 1.2.1. Download the latest version and decompress it on your local machine. Again, like PHPEclipse and the WTP plug-ins, the decompressed file will have two directories, plugins and features. Place the contents of the plugins directory into the plugins directory of the Eclipse installation, and the features directory into Eclipse's features directory. Quit and restart Eclipse to load Eclipse Tidy.

There is one preference we need to configure before we start using Eclipse Tidy. To access Tidy's preferences, go to Windows | Preferences... | HTMLTidy.

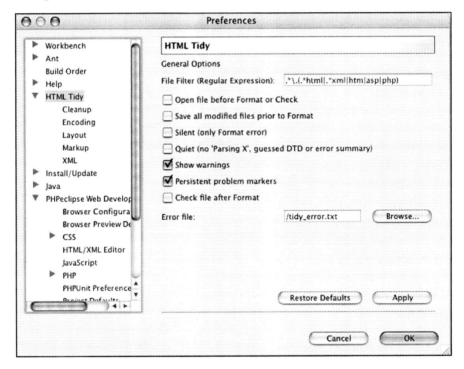

HTML Tidy is highly customizable through a rich set of preferences. The official project site does an excellent job of detailing what each preference does, so we will not get into that here. However, to immediately start working with HTML Tidy, you may need to configure the Error file: on this screen. The error file is the report that HTML Tidy generates. Every HTML error is written to this file. Make sure this file is in a location where you have write permission. By default, HTML Tidy will write to a file called tidy_error.txt. This definitely won't work in Linux or Mac OS X systems since HTML Tidy will try to place the file in the root directory. Changing the path to somewhere in your home directory will definitely work.

Now you can run HTML Tidy on `viewCats.php`. To run HTML Tidy go to the HTML Tidy | Format option or Check option. Format and Check will run the page through the TidyLib and search for errors. They will also both write to the error file. Format, however, will automatically format your code as it sees fit. You may consider this as a warning instead of a feature because it will reformat your nicely formatted code.

When you run HTML Tidy, the errors will appear in a pop up box:

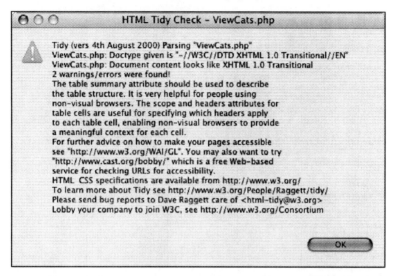

The exact problem and possible fixes are reported. However, this box will only show a limited number of errors and yet is cramped and hard to read. To see all errors in a more readable format, open the error file specified in the preferences. HTML Tidy will also tag the warnings in the left margin of the editor with a warning icon.

Code Documentation Using phpDocumentor

Finally, being good developers, we need to create documentation for our code. phpDocumentor is an excellent open source project that helps us create professional-looking documentation based on code comments. We just need to format our comments in a certain way. phpDocumentor can be downloaded from the official site at `http://www.phpdoc.org/`.

We first need to add comments to our code. The official phpDocumentor site has a concise manual and tutorial to explain how to use phpDocumentor. We will briefly explain the required comment style necessary to build a bare-bones set of documentation.

phpDocumentor operates very similarly to Javadoc. It looks for comment blocks at specific locations. It takes these comment blocks and places them in HTML output. What exactly is documented is divided into three subjects—the page level documentation, the class documentation, and a small block before each function to describe what it does. In the page and class document blocks, the first line is a short description. The second line is a longer description. Method and variable blocks do not have a short description.

Each block must end at the line directly above the class, method, or variable that it is meant to comment on. The exception is the page level block, which must be located right after the <?php tag.

Note there are two lines that begin with the @ symbol. These are phpDocumentor tags. They are used primarily as metadata about the page or class. PHPEclipse has the phpDocumentor tags stored and made available in code assist. You can see this in action by typing @ in a comment block and invoking code assist.

```php
<?php
/**
 *
 * This is the page directive.
 *
 * This is the page code.
 * @author shuchow
 * @version 1.0
 *
 */
/**
 *
 * Short Description of the class.
 *
 * Long Description of the class.
 *
 */
    class Database
    {
        /**
         *
         * This code block will be used to describe $dbConn
         *
         */
        private $dbConn;

        /**
         *
         * This code block will be used to describe getDbConn
         *
         */
        public function getDbConn()
        {
            return $this->dbConn;
        }


    }

?>
```

The example files already have comments included. If you are using PHP 5, be sure to use phpDocumentor 1.3 or greater.

Here are a few commonly used phpDocumentor tags available in PHPEclipse:

Tag	Description
@access	The visibility of a function: private, public, or protected.
@author	The name of the author.
@category	The category of the file.
@global	The datatype and a description of a global variable. Used with @name.
@internal	Internal comments.
@link	A link: the URL followed by a description.
@name	The name of a global variable.
@package	The package that the file belongs in.
@param	A function's parameter datatype and description.
@return	The datatype and a description of a function's return value.
@staticvar	The datatype and a description of a static variable.
@todo	A to-do comment.
@var	The datatype and a description of a common variable.
@version	The version of a file.

phpDocumentor is very easy to install and use. First, make a directory anywhere on your machine that the Apache user has write access to. This is where the generated files will go. This directory does not have to be under the document root, but make sure the Apache user can *write* in it. For Linux and Mac OS X, do this by dropping into the command line and giving write permissions on the directory to everyone by typing in the command `chmod 777 DirectoryName`.

Download the latest release from the project website. Uncompress the package and rename the directory to `phpDoc`. Place the entire `phpDoc` directory in the document root. Part of the application is a web interface to generate the files. With Apache and PHP running, use your web browser and hit this directory. We are going to first tell phpDocumentor which files to parse and then where to output the generated documentation.

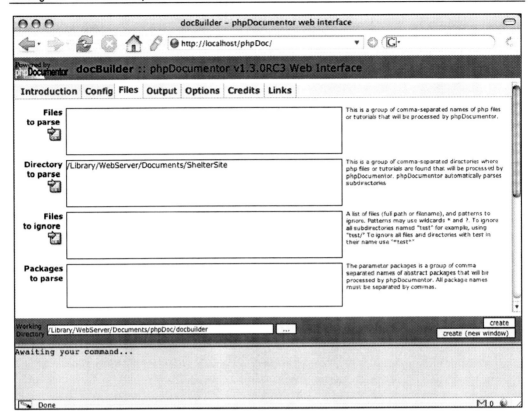

To specify the input files, click on the Files tab of the phpDocumentor web application. Place the full path to the ShelterSite application in the Directory to parse box. As you can see, we have the ability to add or exclude files on an individual basis.

To specify the output location, click on the Output tab:

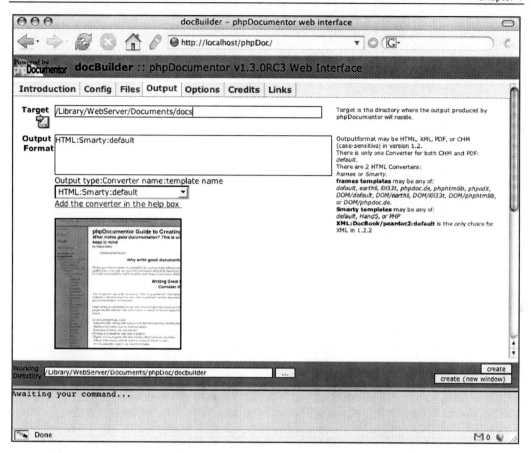

Specify the full path to the output location you created. phpDocumentor includes a set of output template designs for you to choose from. Select one in the template pull-down menu. When you are ready, click on the create button. phpDocumentor will run through the files and build the documentation at the output location:

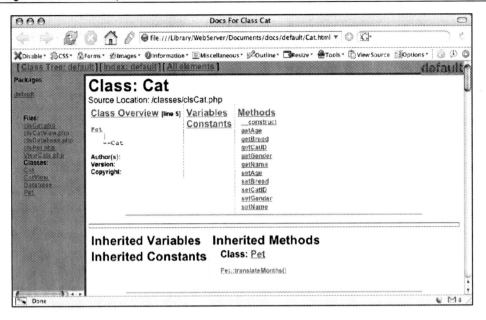

Your documentation is now completed and outputted as HTML files.

Summary

We have now walked through the creation of a basic PHP application using Eclipse, PHPEclipse, and a few other related third-party tools. Our application is a PHP project named ShelterSite that we created in our workspace. We added a few common parts of a web application to the project—class files to hold business logic and database interfacing, view pages to display HTML, and a stylesheet to format our HTML page. In creating our class files, we saw how to use the PHP editor. We saw how code assist helps us in creating code, how the editor visually conveys potential coding problems to us, and how to customize templates. When we encountered a PHP function that we were not sure how to use, we used Eclipse's help system to look up the function's parameters and description.

Installing the Web Tools Platform gave us comprehensive HTML and CSS editors. This set of tools was designed specifically by the Eclipse Foundation to address the needs of web application developers.

Finally, in post-coding work, we saw how PHPEclipse integrates with phpDocumentor to help us create developer documentation for our project. While the WTP does a great job of checking HTML as it is typed, it does not have a minute level of knowledge about the various flavors of HTML and XHTML. Specifically, it does not, nor is it its job to, understand standards compliance. For standards compliance checking, we used the Eclipse Tidy plug-in to check for issues.

At this point, we have enough knowledge to start using Eclipse and PHPEclipse to create any web application. Next, we'll look at extending the basic knowledge that we have gained to help us save time.

5
Testing and Debugging

At various stages of our coding, we will need to make sure that certain parts of our application are working correctly before we can move on to another part. Before we turn our application over to business partners and clients, we will need to test the application as a whole. As bugs are found, we will need to find where the application is breaking in order to fix them. PHPEclipse offers tools to help us do this.

Debugging is the process of identifying what is happening to an application at a certain point. We find where the data and variables went bad and adjust our application to correct this. You probably have done debugging with PHP's echo() or print() functions. By displaying variable values out to the web browser, we can check variable values at certain points of execution in the program. Up to a certain point, this is an effective approach. However, it's fairly limiting in flexibility and most of all, it is time-consuming. It can be very tedious to switch back and forth between the browser and IDE. Moreover, you'll have to set up the echo() statements and often you'll require decision codes (if()) and testing statements (is_array()). Now, you're not only spending time to write debugging code, but you've also cluttered up your application code. When you launch your application into production, be sure to strip out all of your debugging code, or you'll expose embarrassing debugging statements to your customers. However, be careful not to strip out non-debugging code, otherwise your application will break after testing is completed.

IDEs offer a more sophisticated approach to debugging. An often-included feature is a debugger. With a debugger, you can freeze your application at chosen points. You can then evaluate the variables that have been set. You can then unfreeze the application and stop it at another point to evaluate the state changes. You can also alter variable values to test alternative scenarios. This gives you more control and more diagnostic tools quickly and without the need to alter your source code.

In this chapter, we will install, configure, and use a debugger on our system. This debugger will monitor what PHP is doing when it executes scripts. PHPEclipse acts as a client to this debugger. PHPEclipse will translate the debugger's responses into actions in the Eclipse Debug view. We will walk through a debugging session to see the working of basic Eclipse Debug view functions.

> There is a particularly nasty bug in PHPEclipse version 1.1.7 that breaks the ability to see variable values, which we will be examining later in this chapter. Moreover, if you are using Eclipse version 3.1 or higher, you will need PHPEclipse version 1.1.7 or higher. Fortunately, the problem has been fixed in the latest release of PHPEclipse (1.1.8).

About the Debugger

Eclipse's JDT includes a full-featured debugger for Java applications. When Eclipse debugs Java applications, it launches the Debug perspective. From there, you can see details on how your program is executing. The Debug perspective also gives you tools to manipulate your program's execution and see the results.

PHPEclipse integrates Eclipse's Debug perspective with a PHP debugger called PHP Debugger DBG or commonly known as DBG. DBG is a product created by Dmitri Dmitrienko. There are two versions of DBG—a commercial version and an open-source version, which supports less features but is more than sufficient for basic debugging.

DBG works as a PHP extension. It watches the PHP engine. If the engine attempts to execute a PHP script, DBG intercepts this action and watches the traffic between the engine and client. It then returns this to a DBG client.

This setup allows different clients to use DBG since DBG sits between and independent from the PHP engine and client callers. Dmitrienko has released a free UNIX command-line client. The majority of clients that exist are IDEs, like PHPEclipse, that wish to integrate PHP debugging into their product.

Installing the Debugger

Before we can even start to configure Eclipse, we need to prepare our environment. We will need to install and configure DBG to listen to our PHP engine.

First, we need to install DBG. There are precompiled binaries for Windows, Linux, and FreeBSD. The source code is also available for you to download and compile yourself. We may need to do this to install DBG for Mac OS X or if we need to install for a version of PHP that is not officially supported by the binaries.

The second part of this is to configure Eclipse to act as the DBG client. We will set global preferences and application-specific settings.

Before we start, we need a bit of a warning. Installing and configuring the PHPEclipse debugger is not an easy task. We are configuring PHP, Apache, DBG, and PHPEclipse to work together as a unit. It gets even more complicated when we consider container packages for these products like Eclipse, XAMPP, and Marc Liyanage's PHP package. You will need to be meticulous and detailed-oriented. Very often, a typo or a missing trailing slash in a path will cause the whole debugger setup to fail. However, if you're patient and precise, these instructions do work and the benefits of a debugger are a great payoff.

Second, these instructions will assume that you are installing PHP 5. PHP 5 has a directive in the php.ini file, zend.ze1_compatability, which turns on PHP 4 compatibility mode if you need to test PHP 4 code. The instructions for PHP 4 and PHP 5 installations are the same except in two cases—installing precompiled DBG binaries and configuring php.ini files for XAMPP on Windows.

Installing DBG

Installing DBG can be done by installing a precompiled DBG binary, or you can download the source and compile it yourself. If you are running Windows or Linux, consider using a precompiled binary. The only issue for precompiled binaries is whether you are using a version of PHP that is officially supported by DBG. When you download a precompiled binary package, you will see that there is one precompiled binary for every incremental version of PHP. While the DBG project is very good at keeping binaries up to date, there is sometimes a disconnect between the latest version of PHP and the included DBG binaries.

Warning About DBG Precompiled Binaries on Windows

As of this writing, a precompiled version of DBG does not exist for the latest available versions of PHP 4 (4.4.1) and PHP 5 (5.1.1). You can get precompiled binaries for PHP 4.3.x and PHP 5.0.x. The free version of DBG for PHP 5.1.1 and PHP 4.4.1 is scheduled to be released in January 2006. See the thread at `http://support.nusphere.com/ viewtopic.php?t=1759`. You can either buy the commercial version of DBG or use an older version of PHP until then.

If you are using an unsupported version of PHP, or Mac OS X, you will need to compile your own version of DBG. We'll walk through the installation instructions for both cases.

Before we start, we'll need to know where PHP keeps its extensions. The PHP extensions directory is where PHP grabs modules at run time. This directory is defined by the `extension_dir` parameter in your `php.ini` file. By default, this will probably be `'./'`. DBG, however, requires an **absolute path** to be defined here. Accepted convention is to add this to an `ext` or `extensions` directory under their PHP install directory. For example, this can be:

```
extension_dir = \usr\local\php5\ext\
```

If you compiled PHP from source using the previous instructions, the path will be `\usr\local\ php5\ext\`.

If you are using XAMPP, this should already be set to an absolute path. On Windows, it should be set to `\xampp\php\extensions\` (for PHP 4) or `\xampp\php\ext\` (for PHP 5). Make sure you specify the entire path beginning from the directory name.

Whether the directory is already defined or you have defined one, make a note of this directory.

Precompiled Binary Instructions

Follow these instructions to install a precompiled DBG binary for Linux or Windows:

1. Download a DBG package from `http://dd.cron.ru/dbg/downloads.php`. There are several packages available for download on this page. For each platform, you can download a DBGlistener, command-line interface client (CLI), or DBG modules. The modules are the server components, which are what we need. They are further divided into different versions of PHP. Download the correct DBG module version for your version of PHP.

2. Decompress the package and select a binary. The binaries come optimized for 386 and 686 processors. Select the right one for your system. Notice that there is one DBG binary for each incremental version of PHP. Do not take this for granted. DBG can be very picky about having binary versions and PHP versions match up. If you do not see your version of PHP here, follow the instructions for compiling the DBG source code instead.

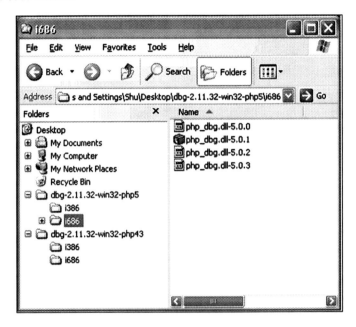

3. Rename the selected binary to php_dbg.dll (for Windows) or php_dbg.so (for Linux). The .dll and .so extensions are standard PHP module extensions for Windows and Linux/Unix systems respectively.

4. Move the php_dbg.dll (or php_dbg.so) to your PHP extensions directory. Move the binary that you renamed in step 3 to the PHP extensions directory defined in php.ini.

This is the last step to install a precompiled DBG binary. You can skip the following instructions to manually compile DBG and jump right to the php.ini configuration section.

Compiling DBG Yourself

If you are using Mac OS X, you will need to compile DBG yourself. You will also need to compile DBG manually if there is no version of DBG that matches your version of PHP.

To compile on Windows, you will need a compiler. The .NET Framework SDK (http://msdn.microsoft.com/netframework/) has a compiler as well as the Visual C++ Toolkit 2003 (http://msdn.microsoft.com/visualc/vctoolkit2003/).

To compile on Mac OS X or Linux, follow these instructions:

1. Download the DBG module source files from `http://dd.cron.ru/dbg/downloads.php`. The source code for the command-line interface client is also available, but we can ignore that package.

2. From the command line, unzip this package and move into the dbg directory.

    ```
    [Blossom:/usr/local/src] shuchow% tar -xvzf dbg-2.32.11.tar.gz…
    [Blossom:/usr/local/src] shuchow% cd dbg-2.32.11
    ```

3. Customize your `deferphpize` script by specifying the location of `phpize`. `deferphpize` is the script used to configure the DBG build. It is located in the newly decompressed dbg directory. Open this file. On line three, the `phpize` variable is set to the location of the `phpize` script. Customize this variable with the specific absolute path to `phpize` script on your installation. `phpize` will probably be in the `bin` directory of your PHP installation.

    ```
    #!/bin/sh

    phpize=${phpize:-"/usr/local/php5C/bin/phpize"}
    if test -f $phpize; then
                $phpize
    ```

4. If you are on Mac OS X, specify `Darwin` in `deferphpize`. Near the top of `deferphpize`, there will be a case statement evaluating the platform. Add `Darwin` as an option to the line with Linux and Solaris.

    ```
    case "$PLAT" in
    FreeBSD)
        libtoolize13 -f -c
        aclocal
        autoconf213
        autoheader213

        ;;
    Linux|SunOS|Darwin)
        aclocal
        ;;
    *)
        echo "unspecified platform"
        exit
        ;;
    esac
    ```

5. Run `deferphpize` and `make`. `deferphpize` will set up the `make` environment; `make` will create the actual binary.

    ```
    Buttercup:/usr/local/src/dbg-2.11.32 root# ./deferphpize
    Configuring for:
    PHP Api Version:        20031224
    Zend Module Api No:     20041030
    Zend Extension Api No:  220040412
    ```

6. After you run `make`, move the `dbg.so` module to the PHP extensions directory. `dbg.so` is the final binary created from this whole process. Move this to the PHP extension directory you specified in `php.ini`.

Configuring php.ini to Use DBG

Now that DBG is in the correct location, we must edit the php.ini file to tell PHP to load and use DBG at script-execution time.

> Remember, if you are using XAMPP with Windows, you will need to make these changes in three php.ini files if you are going to switch between PHP 4 and PHP 5. You will need to edit the active php.ini file at \xampp\apache\bin\php.ini, the PHP 4 template at \xampp\php\php4\php4.ini, and the PHP 5 template at \xampp\php\php5.ini. If you are not going to switch back and forth, you will just need to edit the active php.ini file.

1. Set implicit_flush to On. Find the implicit_flush directive in the file. By default, it should be set to off. Turn this to On.

    ```
    ; Implicit flush tells PHP to tell the output layer to flush itself
    ; automatically after every output block. This is equivalent to
    calling the
    ; PHP function flush() after each and every call to print() or echo()
    and each
    ; and every HTML block. Turning this option on has serious performance
    ; implications and is generally recommended for debugging purposes
    only.
    implicit_flush = On
    ```

2. Add the debugger parameters by adding the following lines to the end of the file. These lines tell PHP to load the DBG extension at run time and passes necessary parameters to the debugger.

    ```
    extension=php_dbg.dll
    [debugger]
    debugger.enabled = true
    debugger.profiler_enabled = true
    debugger.JIT_host = clienthost
    debugger.JIT_port = 7869
    ```

3. Deactivate eAccelerator and Zend Optimizer if installed. If eAccelerator or Zend Optimizer extension is installed, comment out all lines in php.ini that begin with eAccelearator or Zend Optimizer. Do this by placing a semicolon at the beginning of the line. The debugger will not work with eAccelerator. However, since you're installing this on a pure code development machine, speed is not a concern, right? Make sure that the lines below (if present) are commented out:

    ```
    ;extension="eaccelerator.so"
    ;zend_extension="/usr/lib/php4/eaccelerator.so"
    ;zend_extension_ts="/usr/lib/php4/eaccelerator.so"
    ;extension="eaccelerator.dll"
    ;zend_extension_ts="c:\php4\eaccelerator.dll"
    ;zend_extension_manager.optimizer_ts = "\xampp\php\zendOptimizer\lib\
                                            Optimizer"
    ;zend_optimizer.optimization_level=15
    ;zend_extension="c:\php4\eaccelerator.dll"
    ```

Testing Your PHP Installation

At this point, you have installed the DBG debugger and told PHP to load it through the settings in the php.ini file. It's time to see if it has all come together.

Stop and restart Apache. In your browser, pull up the phpinfo() calling page again. DBG should register itself in the copyright notice:

This program makes use of the Zend Scripting Language Engine:
Zend Engine v2.0.3, Copyright (c) 1998-2004 Zend Technologies
with DBG v2.11.32, (C) 2000,2005, by Dmitri Dmitrienko

Powered By

Zend Engine 2

Your page will also now include a separate section for the DBG module. You can see the various features supported by DBG. However, not all of them are supported by the open-source version.

dbg

DBG php debugger, version 2.11.32, Copyright 2001, 2005, Dmitri Dmitrienko, www.nusphere.com

Version	2.11.32
Linked	as a shared library.
Profiler	compiled, enabled

If DBG is loaded, your server set up is now complete. Every time a PHP script executes, DBG will intercept the execution and hold information about the execution. It's now time to set up Eclipse as the client to read and use this information.

Configuring Eclipse as the Debugger Client

PHPEclipse debugger configuration can be divided into two parts.

The first part is specifying the interpreter. In other words, you are telling PHPEclipse where the DBG-enhanced PHP executable is in your system. PHPEclipse passes the debugging file to this binary, listens to the DBG output, and manipulates Eclipse to give you feedback on what the PHP script is doing.

The second part is to create a debugging configuration for the file you want to test.

Specifying an Interpreter

To specify an interpreter, go to Windows | Preferences | PHPeclipse Web Development | PHP | Installed Interpreters.

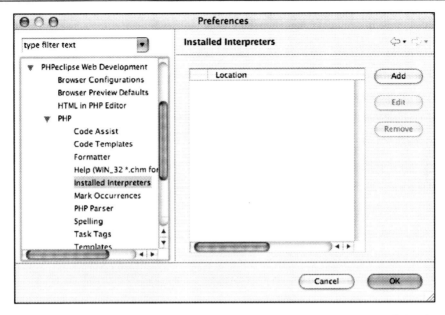

Click on the Add button to add a new interpreter. This will bring up an Open File dialog box.

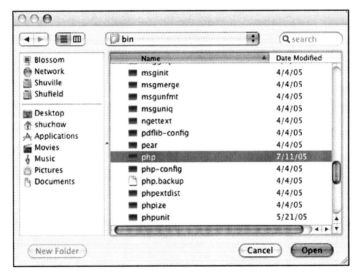

Using this dialog box, specify the absolute path to the PHP binary.

If you are using XAMPP, use the PHP executable in the \xampp\apache\bin\ directory (for example, c:\apachefriends\xampp\apache\bin\) as opposed to the one in the \xampp\php\ directory. The \apache\bin\ directory is also where the active php.ini file resides.

If you are using the Entropy PHP package, the binary is located in \usr\local\php5\bin\ for PHP 5 or \usr\local\php\bin\ for PHP 4.

Creating a Debugging Configuration

This is the final step in getting the debugger working. We need to create the testing parameters and settings. Each file you wish to debug will get its own set of parameters and settings. In Java debugging, these settings allow us to experiment with the execution environment, or recreate a JVM environment that is closer to our production server. Most of the debugging parameters available for tweaking are irrelevant in PHP. However, debugging configurations in PHPEclipse are still necessary. The few PHPEclipse debugging settings that are available allow us to experiment a little bit without changing our code. Even if we do not wish to alter debugging parameters, Eclipse still needs a configuration to debug an application.

Each configuration is tied to a single PHP file. We will need to create a file to debug before we can set up a configuration for it. Create a simple PHP file in our ShelterSite project. Name it debug.php and enter this code:

```php
<?php
  $a = 1;
  $b = 2;
  $a = 5;
?>
```

As we go through this chapter, we'll encounter small snippets of code to demonstrate debugging features and principles. All of these snippets are included in the example debug.php file available in the code download for this chapter. Each snippet is commented out with an explanation of which feature it demonstrates. To follow along, you can either type these snippets into your Eclipse environment, or copy-paste them from the example debug.php file.

In the left margin of the debugger, double-click on the area next to line number 5 to set a breakpoint. Breakpoints tell the application to stop executing right before evaluating the line of code. In essence, this freezes the program. When frozen, we can examine the program's state. We can examine variable values and method execution. After stopping, we can choose to continue executing the program or execute it one line at a time to further investigate how the program runs.

Breakpoints appear as blue dots in the margin. You can also set breakpoints by right-clicking on the margin and selecting **Toggle PHP Breakpoint**.

This script sets two variables, changes one of them, and has a breakpoint. While very rudimentary, it gives us a chance to test the debugger's ability to stop at a breakpoint and monitor variable values. If these two functions work, we can conclude that our setup of the debugger has been successful. In this script, we now have a target for a debugging configuration. Debugging configurations are set in the Run | Debug... menu option. Click on Debug to bring up the Debug configuration and management screen.

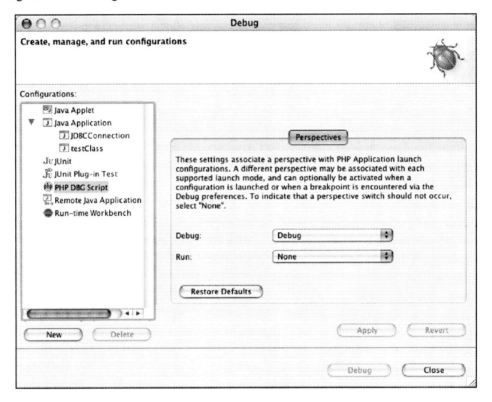

We are going to debug a PHP application using the DBG debugger, so select PHP DBG Script and click on the New button. In future, you can return to this screen to delete or change settings for a configuration.

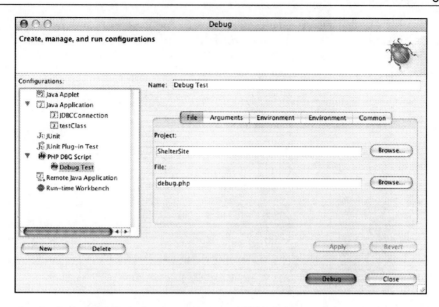

The File tab asks for specific information about the file you wish to debug. Give this configuration a name in the Name field. Specify the project and file in their respective fields. You can manually type them in or click the Browse... buttons to find the items. We can safely skip configuring the Arguments tab for now, but we should be aware of it and take a look at it:

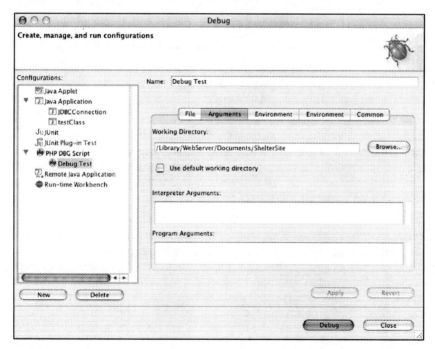

Working Directory is pre-filled, but not used. This tab asks for interpreter parameters and file input parameters. If you are doing PHP command-line scripting, you can add arguments here. Click on the first Environment tab to continue (there are two Environment tabs, with the first tab for general settings and the second one for configuring environment variables):

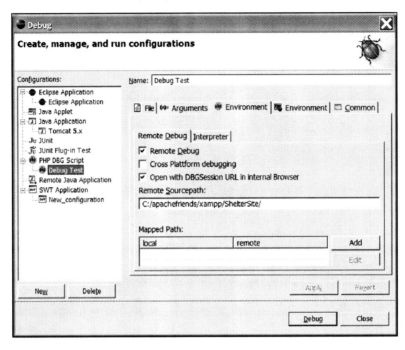

In the Environment tab, the Remote Debug tab should appear first by default. Make sure the Remote Debug and Open with DBGSession URL in internal Browser checkboxes are checked. In Remote Sourcepath, specify the absolute path to the directory where your debug subject is located.

> Make sure there is a trailing slash at the end of your entry! Otherwise, the script location will not be recognized. The debugger will appear to run, but it will not register any variables and will not stop at breakpoints. These are the most common debugger problems reported by people on PHPEclipse forums, and the vast majority of the time, it is because of this missing end slash.

Remote debugging is the process of debugging a file on another server. The server must have DBG installed and running. In PHPEclipse debugging, we fool Eclipse by treating our local PHP/Apache instance as a remote server. As of this writing, true remote debugging support in PHPEclipse is in its infant stages, but it can be done. First, since the source code files are on a different server, you will need to mount the share locally. In PHPEclipse, configure this mapping with the Mapped Path fields. If there is a discrepancy between the operating system that you are using and the server's operating system, for example, using Windows and accessing a Linux server, select the Cross Platform debugging checkbox.

Proceed with configuration of your local debugging environment by clicking on the Interpreter tab.

In Mac OS X, as of PHPEclipse 1.1.8, a bug exists that prevents the entire label of installed interpreters to appear. Just click on the white box next to the Remote Debug tab to pull up the Interpreter tab.

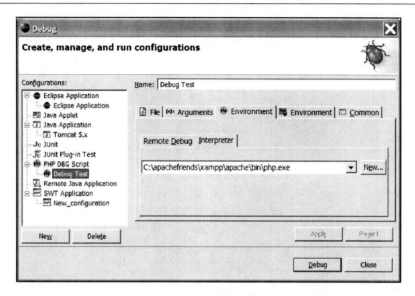

Select the interpreter from the pull-down menu. This is the same interpreter as you installed in the preferences earlier. By allowing you to specify an interpreter, PHPEclipse allows you to experiment with different settings. You can install different versions of PHP with different compile parameters and test your application against them.

At this point, you have finished building your debugging configuration. Press the Apply button to save the configuration. Click on the Debug button to begin the debugging process. You can quickly access this configuration from the Debug icon in the Eclipse toolbar, which holds your most recent configurations, or press *Ctrl* (*Command* on a Mac) +*F11*, which automatically debugs your last configuration. You'll notice that when you debug, very often it's a repeating cycle of debug, quick edit, debug, quick edit. You'll be thankful for having such quick access to your debugging configuration.

If you are not in the Debug perspective, Eclipse will switch over to the Debug perspective and may ask you if you want to do this. Click Yes to accept this change:

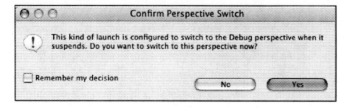

In the Debug perspective, Eclipse will pass your file to PHP and debugging will begin:

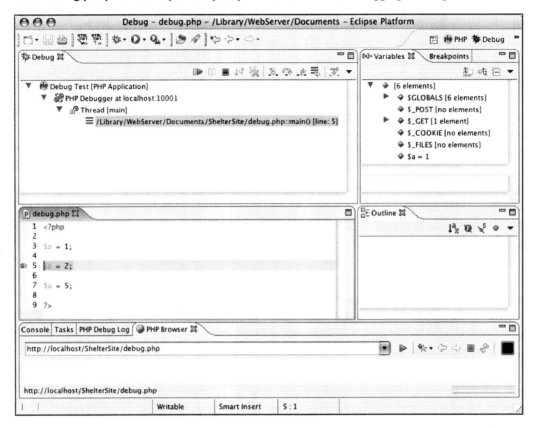

The process will run until the first breakpoint, which we set to line five, and then stop to await further orders. We have several visual clues that let us know that this is happening.

- In the Debug view, we see that the debugger has started, spawned a thread called main() (which is a residual effect from Java firing main() functions at launch), and the stack is in progress at line five.

- In the editor, line five is highlighted, and a break arrow overlays the breakpoint on line five. This highlight and break arrow tell us where the program is in the process.

- In the Variables view, we see that this view is actually keeping track of variables and their values.

If these three things happen, we know our debugger is working and PHPEclipse is configured correctly. We can begin to debug our PHP applications.

Troubleshooting Tips

Correctly calibrating all of software packages that make up the debugger can be tricky. There's a chance that the debugger will fail on the first run. Usually, the debugging process will execute the script successfully, but the Variables view will be empty and the debugger will not stop at breakpoints. Unfortunately, Eclipse will not give out any further details except for Java exception errors in the Error Log view. Follow these general tips to debug your debugger:

1. Make sure DBG is installed correctly. If DBG is not even registering in your `phpinfo()` page, then that needs to be fixed first. No amount of Eclipse configuration will correct the situation.

2. If DBG is installed correctly, chances are your problem is in the PHPEclipse configuration or `php.ini/httpd.conf` configuration. Although not impossible, it is probably not an Eclipse error, nor, as long as it's reported as active in the `phpinfo()` page, a problem with DBG.

3. Delete almost everything in your `configuration` directory except for the `config.ini` file. This directory holds your configuration settings for Eclipse. It may have been corrupted. When removed, Eclipse will automatically build everything except your `config.ini` file, which is critical for Eclipse to startup. The drawback to this method is that you will have to reconfigure a lot of your Eclipse preferences.

4. Ask for help using all available resources. For each of the open-source products you are configuring, there are several avenues of communication with developers and other users. Sure, there is overlap and conflict with each method. A project may have a BBS forum on the site, a BBS forum at SourceForge, a bug tracker at SourceForge, a user mailing list, and a developer mailing list. Check the archives of all of these tools. Very often, someone else will have run across the same problem and have been able to fix the problem.

5. If your debugger was working correctly and has suddenly stopped working, or the debugger works on some files and not others, beware of files that finish executing. In PHPeclipse, the Debug view will not add a <terminated> signal to finished programs as it will in Java applications. Moreover, variables will set themselves correctly and then clear themselves from the Variables view! This means that the debugger may actually be working correctly and the script has either finished executing or encountered a `die()` function. In fact, in the example `debug.php` file, you'll see that each code block has a `die()` call at the end where we set our final breakpoint. This is to show us the final state of the application right before the execution ends. If we allowed the execution to finish, the application's variables would be wiped from the Variables view. The best and most reliable way to see if your debugger is working correctly is whether it stops at a breakpoint.

6. Use the Error Log view. Eclipse has a very extensive and useful error logging feature. If the initial debugger run does not seem to work, it probably logged one or more lines in the Error Log.

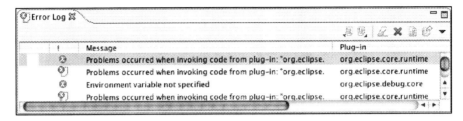

Each exception will throw an error. Of particular importance are the Export Log and Open Log buttons. These features will collect all of the exceptions into either one text file or a window on screen. If you feel that your error is a bug in either PHPEclipse or Eclipse, gather the information in this log and post it to the bug forum of the appropriate project. Before you collect the exceptions, be sure to wipe out all existing entries in the Error Log view using the Delete Log button in the view's toolbar. Then, when you recreate the error, the log you send with your report will be free of errors that are unrelated to the bug.

How to Use the Debugger

By clicking on the Debug button, we have started a debugging session. Eclipse automatically switches us to the Debug perspective. The application begins to execute, but it stops at line five because we told it to stop via a breakpoint. Our program is now frozen until we do something to advance it. Before we advance, let's take a look around the Debug perspective, explore the views, and see how things are frozen when our program has stopped.

Debug View

The Debug view gives us a good idea of what the application is doing. Mainly it tells us what function the application is executing at that particular breakpoint:

The Debug view organizes things from the broadest in scope to the most specific. The first line, the Project takes its name from the name of the debugging configuration. The Debug Target is the container for the threads that are running. Underneath the Debug Target are the executing threads. Since PHP is a single-threaded language, only one thread, the Main Thread, will ever execute at one time. This thread executes functions whose **frames** appear as a **call stack**. The call stack, with all the frames, is listed underneath the Main Thread.

Frames and call stacks may be new concepts to a web developer, so we'll briefly explain them. When a function or method gets invoked, the system allocates a certain amount of memory to hold variables and do work for that function. This memory is called a frame. If a function calls another function, a second frame is created and stacked on top of the first frame. This second frame needs to execute and finish before it is removed from the stack. The first frame then continues with its execution. If more functions are called, they are placed at the top of the call stack.

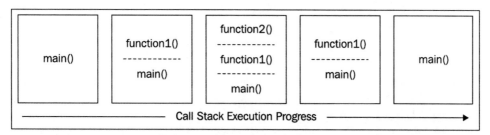

In PHPEclipse, the execution of the full script is treated as the `main()` function and is labeled as such. If you've worked with C, C++, or Java, you'll know that a function named `main()` in a class holds special significance. The system will automatically fire off `main` to execute a program.

In our example, we see that the Eclipse has started work on the script and stopped at line five of the page. This is shown in the first and only frame. Frames are represented as three horizontal blue bars in the Debug view. If we had called another function and stopped inside of it, we would see another set of frames on top of main. Collectively, all of the frame lines underneath the main thread line represent the call stack of our script.

By reporting on the call stack, the Debug view not only lets us know where we are in a script, but also how we got there. We can trace back the calling functions and see what was called. As we add loops and conditions into our application, seeing the breadcrumb trail is helpful to the debugging process.

The Debug view also lets us execute through the application using icons in the toolbar. They are listed below:

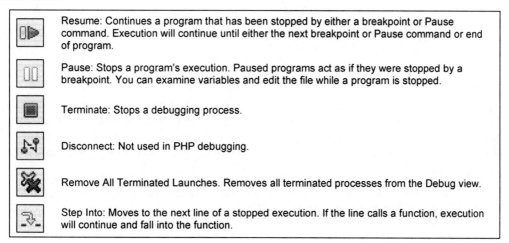

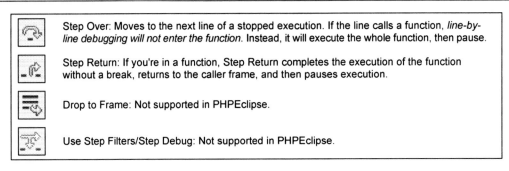

	Step Over: Moves to the next line of a stopped execution. If the line calls a function, *line-by-line debugging will not enter the function*. Instead, it will execute the whole function, then pause.
	Step Return: If you're in a function, Step Return completes the execution of the function without a break, returns to the caller frame, and then pauses execution.
	Drop to Frame: Not supported in PHPeclipse.
	Use Step Filters/Step Debug: Not supported in PHPeclipse.

We'll see how these navigation features work later, when we start an actual debugging session.

Variables View

With the Variables view, we can see the exact values of all variables at any breakpoint. Many consider this to be one of the most valuable tools in an IDE. No longer do you have to echo out variables to the screen. You can evaluate them as the program runs, get far more information quickly, and alter the values if need be. You even have more flexibility to evaluate more complex variables. Object properties are listed in the Variables view. There is no need to output properties one by one. With arrays, all keys and values are reported. You no longer have to loop through arrays in a foreach loop to examine values.

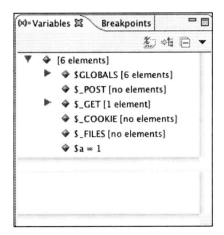

In this example, we see that the variable $a was set to a value of 1. We also see a few environment variables that were set by the web server environment and reported back in DBG. The breakpoint is set to line five, which is where $b is set to a value of 2. Remember, breakpoints are honored right *before* the line of code is executed. If the breakpoint was set to line six, we would see $b = 2 in the Variables view.

The Variables view offers several display options in its toolbar. However, these are designed to work with Java variables and do not work in PHPeclipse.

Breakpoints View

The Breakpoints view lists all breakpoints in a workspace. If you have a Java project with breakpoints, they will also appear here. Each entry gives you the file and line number:

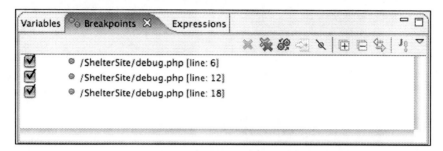

This view's toolbar gives you some global management functions of your breakpoints:

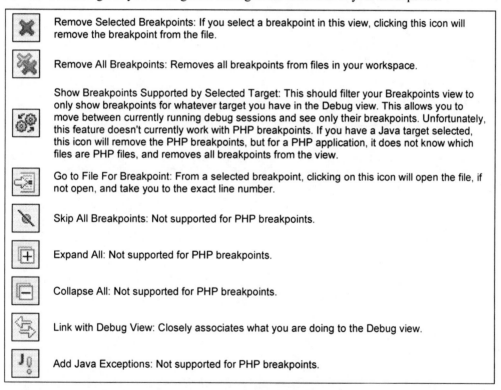

Console, Editor, Outline, and PHP Browser

All four views are part of this perspective and are helpful in the debugging process. You can edit files on the fly in the middle of a debugging session and fix reported errors immediately. The Outline gives you an overview of your file. The PHP Browser will show you the requested file.

The only difference is the editor. The editor is linked directly with the debugging session. You've already seen the breakpoints represented by blue dots in the editor. During the debugging session, when the debugger encounters a breakpoint, a breakpoint flag will appear over the breakpoint and the line will be highlighted. This is another way Eclipse shows you exactly where the execution has stopped.

When you move through the file, the breakpoint flag and line highlighting will follow you. They represent the stopping point of your application.

Navigating Through a Debugging Session

If you haven't stopped the previous debugging session, do so now. In the Debug view, click on the Terminate button in the toolbar. The Debug target line will now have <terminated> at the beginning and the icon will lose its motion arrows, indicating that the process has stopped. Click on this motionless Debug target line to highlight it and click on Remove All Terminated Launches to remove it from the view.

Let us try a slightly more complicated debugging exercise. Now that we have a familiarity with the Debug perspective and what we're looking at, let's try to navigate through a session. Debugging in PHPEclipse follows industry-common practices and works very similarly to debugging in other IDEs. The terms you encounter here can be carried over to other languages and other tools.

First, replace the code in debug.php with this code. This code sets some variables, and calls a local function. The local function returns a value that is used by the calling method.

```php
<?php

$catID = 1;
$catName = "Crinkle";
$catID = 42;

$hb = getHairball("Gack");

echo $catName . " presents a hairball!\r" . $hb;

function getHairball($sound)
{
  $size = 6;
  $sound = " *Urp* ";
```

```
    $hairball = str_repeat($sound, $size);

    return $hairball;
}
    die("End of Script");
?>
```

Set a breakpoint at line four, where $catName is set to 'Crinkle'.

Fire off the debug session again by going to the Run | Debug History | Debug Test menu option. You can also find the Debug History function in the toolbar of Eclipse.

The debugger will start and stop at line four. The only line that has been executed is line three, where we set $catID to 1. Confirm the value of $catID in the Variables view.

Click on the Step Into button to advance execution to the next line. Now, line four has completely executed and $catName has been set. Confirm both the $catID and $catName variables values in the Variables view.

Click on Step Into again. Line five has executed. The debugger will skip line six, a blank line, and stop at line seven. The value of $catID has changed. Again, confirm this in the Variables view. $catID should have shown up previously as 1, but now line five should have changed it to 42. This is how your Variables view should look like right now:

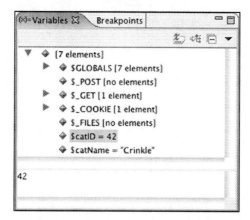

Clicking on the variable will give us the entire value of the variable in the lower value pane. This pane is useful for values that are extraordinarily long.

Click on Step Into again. This time, Step Into truly steps into a function. The debugger will stop at the first line of the function. A second frame is created in the Debug view's call stack. The frame is named after the called function. The Variables view only shows variables that are in scope. When the debugger enters a function, the Variables view shows the local variables of the function that it is executing. However, Eclipse by has no means forgotten the variables in the script that called the function. At any time, you can see the parent's stack variable values by clicking on the preceding call stack in the Debug view. The Variables view will change to show only the values for that particular stack. You can move up the stacks indefinitely with this method to see all variable values. To return to the function's variables, click on the function's call stack in the Debug view:

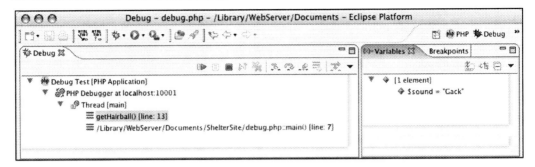

Press Step Into three more times to advance to line 17, the return statement. All three variables within getHairball() should be set including $hairball, which will be returned and stored in $hb. Press Step Into one more time. The debugger will exit the function and pick up exactly right after the line where it entered the function. In this case, the debugger goes to line nine.

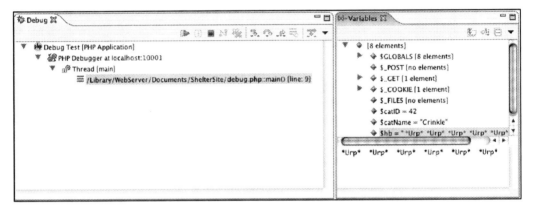

All the variables have been set. Click on Terminate and Remove on the toolbar to quit and clear this debugging session.

We just ran through the entire script line by line and saw how our variables change and how PHP navigates through an application. Let's see how the other two navigation commands, Step Over and Step Return, work.

The Step Over button is used to step over a function invocation in the debugging session. The function still executes, and any changes to the application still occur. Since the process stops at a line before it executes it, Step Over works in a line where a function is called. The calling function moves to the next line of code to be executed after it returns from the function.

See this in action by executing the Debug test session again. From the very beginning, instead of clicking Step Into, press Step Over. Even though the first line does not have code that executes a function, Step Over still advances. Its job is to move to the next line in the function, and nothing fancier. Press Step Over twice after line four to get to line seven, where we encounter the call to getHairball(). Last time, we pressed Step Into to move into this function, but this time, press Step Over instead. The debugger will execute the function, but you will not be taken into the function.

You'll see that the screen is exactly the same as if we just exited the program via a series of Step Into's like from the last example. Step Over is helpful if you just want to test the output of a function, or if you are confident that the function works and the problem lies elsewhere.

If you move into a large function and debugging it has become tedious, you can exit out of the function using the Step Return command. Step Return will continue executing the function, but the debugger will exit out of the function and return to the calling function.

For all practical purposes, PHP treats include files as if they were part of the script at the point where the `include()`, `require()`, or `require_once()` function is called. Functions that are declared in include files are stored in memory as the script reads their container include file, and the functions are available for calling later on in the main script or other include files. If you debug a script that has functions declared in external include files, PHP and the debugger will treat those functions the same as functions declared in the main script. In other words, regardless of how many include files you have, and how many functions are declared in those include files, PHP will know about the include files, and their contents. The debugger client will move to the functions in include files, and Step Into, Step Over, and Step Return will work exactly the same way as in one large script, even though you may have many functions declared outside of the script in include files.

Debugging Strategies

Now that we've successfully navigated through the application, let's take a look at some more useful features of the debugger, and how we can use them to solve common problems that we face.

Working with Variables

The Variables view is not limited to outputting simple key/value pairs. It also gives us information on more complex objects.

Debugging Arrays

Arrays can be complicated beasts. Throw in variables as indexes, looping, and multi-dimensional arrays and they become even more complicated. Even the standard echoing of variables is not easy because often, it's hard to figure out what you want to display. Fortunately, the Variables view handles them with ease.

Consider this code:

```php
<?php

    $myArray = array();
    $myArray[0] = "Zero";
    $myArray[1] = "One";
?>
```

We declare an array and give it two elements. The Variables view will nest the individual elements underneath the array like this:

Multi-dimensional arrays are basically single arrays nested in parent single arrays. Thus, the Variables view will nest the second array underneath the first array. This code shown below:

```php
<?php

    $myArray = array();
    $myArray[0][0] = "Zero and Zero";
    $myArray[0][1] = "Zero and One";
    $myArray[1][0] = "One and Zero";
    $myArray[1][1] = "One and One";
?>
```

will produce this output in the Variables view:

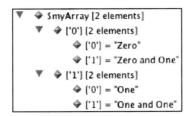

If your key or index is a variable, the Variables view reports back on the key and array value. This makes it extremely helpful when there are frequent key changes, for example, in a loop.

```php
<?php

    $myArray = array();
    $key = "Zero";
    $myArray[$key] = 0;
    $key = "One";
    $myArray[$key] = 1;
    $key = "Two";
    $myArray[$key] = 2;
?>
```

If you step through the application, you will see the $key variable take the value of Zero, One, and eventually, Two. If we set a breakpoint at $key = "Two" our Variables view would look like this:

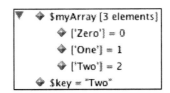

This example also shows us how the Variables view handles associative arrays. Again, the main array is listed as an element. Each item is nested under in a tree-like manner.

Debugging Objects

The Variables view also gives you good and complete information on objects. Properties are displayed for each instantiated object. Consider this code block:

```php
<?php

    require_once("classes/clsCat.php");
```

```
$catObj = new Cat();
$catObj->setName("Roman");
$catObj->setGender("Male");
$catObj->setBreed("Orange Tabby DSH");

?>
```

This code block instantiates a Cat object in our project and sets a few properties via the setter methods as seen here in the Variables view.

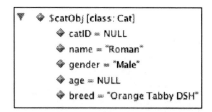

Similar to the array structure, the Variables view nests properties underneath the container object. However, the type of object (in this case, a Cat) is displayed for you next to the variable name. Since an object reserves memory space when instantiated, we can see that the properties that were not set are still reported, but have the value of NULL.

Changing Variable Values

With any variable, you can change its value in the middle of debugging. You may want to do this to test a specific reaction from your program to a new value, inject test data that will come from an external source, or override errors caused somewhere else in the program. Let's see how this works by adding the following three lines to the end of the previous code block where we created a cat and named him Roman. We'll add a breakpoint at the line where $output is set.

```
$catObj->setAge("60");
$ageString = $catObj->getAge() . " months old";
$output = "The cat's name is " . $catObj->getName() . ". Age: " . $ageString;
```

When executed, the program will recreate the cat object and set the parameters. This time, an age is set, and an age string is set. However, 60 months old cat sounds awkward. Let's change that.

```
▼  ◆ $catObj [class: Cat]
        ◆ catID = NULL
        ◆ name = "Roman"
        ◆ gender = "Male"
        ◆ age = "60"
        ◆ breed = "Orange Tabby DSH"
   ◆ $ageString = "60 months old"
```

To change a variable, double-click on it in the Variables view. You can also right-click on the variable name and select Change Value...

This will bring up the Set Value window. You can enter any value here. Be aware that any value you enter here will be considered a string. If you test the changed variable for data types later on in the application, any test except for is_string() will return false.

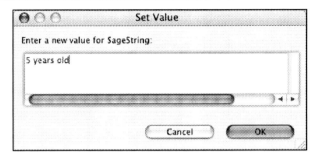

Resume the debugging session. At the end of the script, we see the new value of $ageString, and we see the new value used in the creation of $output:

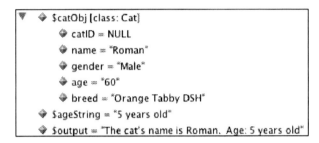

Forms, Cookies, Session, and Server Variables

As web developers, we frequently work with GET, POST, cookie, and session variables in our applications. We also often use environment variables specific to our web server. For example, we might need to grab the name of the server to determine if we're running in a development or production environment.

PHP tracks all of these external variables in **superglobal arrays**. You're probably familiar with using $_GET, $_POST, $_COOKIE, $_SESSION, or $_SERVER to access these variables. The Java debugger allows you to add environment variables to the debugging process. This can be found in the Environment tab when you create a debugging configuration. Unfortunately, PHPEclipse's debugger does not yet support this. Since we're working with pure code, we also cannot trigger a form submission, because we simply cannot see a physical button in our source code. However, we can still debug any applications that rely on this information.

Remember that the Variables view has no problem handling arrays and objects. Fortunately, these external variables are placed in associative arrays by PHP. Knowing this, we can fool the debugger into thinking that variables it encounters during the debugging session are part of these arrays. Our strategy is to add the necessary variables to the appropriate array at the top of the page. Essentially, this is stub data solely used for the purpose of testing the page.

The $_SERVER variables are handled slightly differently. PHP already has all of this information. We just need to trigger the Variables view into displaying them. This can be done by simply referencing any of the $_SERVER variables or declaring an empty $_SERVER variable into the array.

Let's see an example of how this would work. Let's create a small, hypothetical action page. Let's assume that a form page elsewhere will use this action page as the action in its form tag. This page uses $_POST variables to create an SQL statement. This SQL statement could be used to insert the form fields into their appropriate column in the database. Enter this code into a file named catAction.php.

```php
<?php

    $_SERVER[] = "";
    $_POST['Name'] = "Boo";
    $_POST['Gender'] = "Male";
    $_POST['Age'] = "84";
    $_POST['Breed'] = "Domestic Long Hair";

    if ($_SERVER['REQUEST_METHOD'] == "POST")
    {
      insertCat($_POST['Name'], $_POST['Gender'], $_POST['Age'],
      $_POST['Breed']);
    }
    else
    {
      die("A general error has occured. Please use your back button to go back
          one page and try this again.");
    }

    function insertCat($name, $gender, $age, $breed)
    {
      $sql = "INSERT INTO tCat (Name, Gender, Age, Breed) VALUES
      ('" . $name . "', '" . $gender . "', " . $age . ", '" . $breed . "')";

      //Do database stuff here.
    }

?>
```

This is a typical example of what a form processing page would do. The key difference is the first five lines where we're setting some variables into the superglobal array. In this example we're setting POST variables, but you can also set cookie, session, and GET variables. The first line will trigger the $_SERVER array to show in the Variables view. Technically, this is not required in our example page because the test in the if statement will trigger the $_SERVER array. However, we include it here as an example if you need to see these variables in a page that would not normally use them.

Set a breakpoint at the line $_POST['Breed'] = "Domestic Long Hair"; This will stop the execution and we can examine the new variables. Create a new debugging configuration for this page and start a debugging session.

```
▼  ◆ $_POST [3 elements]
       ◆ ['Name'] = "Boo"
       ◆ ['Gender'] = "Male"
       ◆ ['Age'] = "84"
```

Notice that now the $_POST array has three elements (with the fourth, Breed, not being declared yet). Prior to this, the $_POST array has been empty. Since the debugger can only send GET requests to Apache, POST variables never exist. This will pose a problem in the first conditional test. As a rudimentary security precaution, we make sure that the browser is sending a POST request. If a GET request occurs, we display an error.

Fortunately, we can also get around this request method enforcement now that the $_SERVER variables are displayed. Find the $_SERVER['REQUEST_METHOD'] variable in the Variables view. You can see that the default is GET. Any displayed variable is subject to our manipulation. We can change this value to POST. When we continue executing, PHP will read the changed value of $_SERVER['REQUEST_METHOD'], see that it's POST, and allow the insertCat() function to be called.

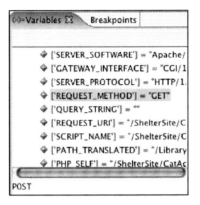

If you Step Into the rest of the application, you can see that the REQUEST_METHOD test passes successfully, and the POST variables are passed correctly into the insertCat() function:

```
▼  ◆  [4 elements]
      ◆ $name = "Boo"
      ◆ $gender = "Male"
      ◆ $age = "84"
      ◆ $breed = "Domestic Long Hair"
```

Using this variable injection technique, we can now debug all of our applications that rely on external variables.

Watching Variables

As of the beta versions of PHPEclipse version 1.1.8, PHPEclipse supports variable watching. This feature allows us to tell Eclipse to watch particular variables and tell us their values no matter where we are. When a variable is watched, it and its value will always be reported in the Expressions view. If the value gets changed, its updated value will be reported in the Expressions view. In a way, this is a filter for the Variables view, which reports on all variables.

We will demonstrate this feature with this block of code:

```
$gidgetWeight = 5;
$gidgetWeight = eat($gidgetWeight);
$gidgetWeight = eat($gidgetWeight);
$gidgetWeight = eat($gidgetWeight);
settype($gidgetWeight, "string");

function eat($weight)
{
    return $weight + 5;
}
```

To set a variable watch, we must first catch the variable. Set a breakpoint at the first line after where the variable is first used. In this example, we will watch the variable named gidgetweight. Set the breakpoint at the second line, where the eat() function is called for the first time. Execute the debugger and it will stop at the breakpoint. In the Variables view, we see that $gidgetweight has been set with a value of 5. Right-click on $gidgetweight in the Variables view and select Watch:

This will place $gidgetweight in the Expressions view:

Use Step Over to go through the script. In the Expressions view, you will see gidgetweight go from 5, to 10, to 15, to 20 with each call to eat(). In the last expression, we change the type of gidgetweight to a string. If you have the Show Type Names option in the Expressions toolbar turned on, you will see the type of gidgetweight go from long to string.

The other options available in the Expressions toolbar are as follows:

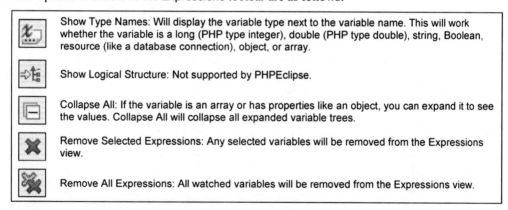

There is another way to watch an expression. You can tell the Expressions view to watch for a variable name. If the debugger encounters a variable with the watched name, it will report its value in the Expressions view. To do this, set the breakpoint before gidgetweight is called and run the debugger. With the debugger stopped, right-click anywhere in the Expressions view and select Add Watch Selection from the contextual menu. A dialog box will appear that lets you add the name of the variable to the watch list.

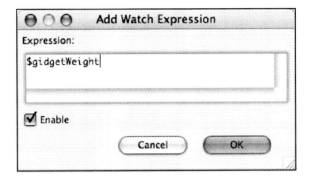

Type in the name of the variable you wish to watch. Make sure you add the dollar sign. Click on the OK button to add this variable to the watch list. Now, when the variable is declared and a value is set, it will appear in the Expressions view and will be watched normally. This method is helpful in determining if a variable is even set during the execution of a script.

Run

Another tool available for us is the Run command. Run works similarly to and closely with Debug. Both share the same configuration settings window. The settings are accessed from the Run | Run... menu option. Whatever files you configured for debugging are available in Run.

Run will execute the program with no stopping at breakpoints, and you cannot step through lines. Its differences from Debug make it useful in several key situations.

- Run will execute the file as if it is a web browser requesting a page. If you send a web page through Run, it will be displayed as a web page in PHP Browser view. Debug will also do this, but only if you do not stop execution.

- If you are developing a command-line PHP application, Run can save you from a lot of 'alt-tabbing'. You do not have to switch over to a terminal to launch your program. You can execute it from Eclipse.

- Run will write output to the Console view. PHP errors, echo(), and print() statements will appear. Run will also pass and output arguments sent to the PHP interpreter via the Arguments tab in the configuration menu:

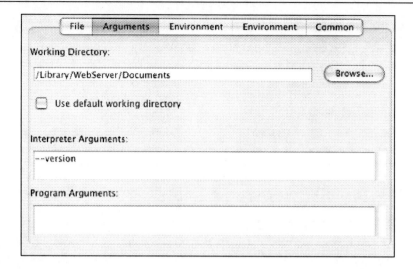

XDebug

Currently, the PHPEclipse team is working on debugging interface for XDebug, another PHP debugger similar to DBG. This will give you a choice of debuggers to use. This may not appear important right now since PHPEclipse will be your client to both debuggers. However, this is important if you have other types of clients hitting your PHP development servers. These other clients may not be able to communicate with DBG or vice versa. Down the road, there may be feature disparities between the two debuggers. Supporting both will make sure PHPEclipse continues to be a useful and relevant PHP IDE.

In this section, we will take a look at how PHPEclipse will interface with XDebug. This will require two key components: the PHPEclipse/XDebug plug-ins and the XDebug shared module installed on our copy of PHP.

For the former, XDebug support is slated for inclusion in PHPEclipse version 1.1.8. As of this writing, it is currently available in the HEAD of PHPEclipse's CVS repository, but still very experimental. If 1.1.8 has not been officially released, you will need to compile your own set of PHPEclipse plug-ins in order to get XDebug support and to do the tasks that we will walk through. To build PHPEclipse yourself, follow the instructions at `http://www.plog4u.org/index.php/ Developing_PHPeclipse:Developing_Process`. If you have installed the snapshot binary installation of 1.1.8, that version currently does not have XDebug support. You will still need to build PHPEclipse yourself.

Building your own version of PHPEclipse is beyond the scope of this book. If you need to do so, it also means that XDebug support is not stable enough for a CVS snapshot release. It may cause Eclipse to behave strangely and may even result in data loss. Therefore, if XDebug is not present in your version of PHPEclipse, it would be wiser just to read through this section.

Installing XDebug

Like DBG, XDebug requires installation of a shared PHP module. To download XDebug, go to http://www.xdebug.org. Along the right navigation bar are several versions of XDebug. PHPEclipse supports version 2.0, which is currently in second beta.

Windows Installation

XDebug.org has DLL files already precompiled for Windows. The installation of this file mimics the method of installation of the DLL file for DBG. In order to use the precompiled versions of XDebug, download the appropriate version for your version of PHP. Place this version in your PHP extensions directory, the same one that you installed the DBG module. XDebug is less tied to your PHP version than DBG. Therefore, you should not need to compile XDebug for Windows.

Mac OS X/Linux Installation

Mac OS X and Linux will need XDebug compiled from source. The compile procedure is similar to that of DBG. We will reference the deferphpize module, then compile and make the source code:

1. Download the DBG module source files from http://www.xdebug.org. Be sure to grab XDebug 2.0. The source code to the clients is also available, but they can be ignored.

2. From the command line, unzip this package and move into the directory.

    ```
    [Blossom:/usr/local/src] shuchow% tar -xvzf xdebug-  2.0.0.beta2.tgz
    [Blossom:/usr/local/src] shuchow% cd xdebug-2.0.0beta2
    ```

3. From the XDebug source directory, run phpize. This is a script that exists in the same directory as your PHP binary. This is the bin directory underneath your PHP installation. You may need to specify the absolute path to phpize. In Entropy, this will be /usr/local/php5/bin/phpize.

    ```
    [Blossom:/usr/local/src/xdebug-2.0.0beta2] shuchow%
    /usr/local/php5/bin/phpize
    ```

4. Configure with –enable-xdebug and –with-php-config. php-config is a script that is also in your PHP bin directory. When compiling, you will need to enable XDebug and specify the location of php-config.

    ```
    [Blossom:/usr/local/src/xdebug-2.0.0beta2] shuchow% ./configure –enable-
    xdebug –with-php-config=/usr/local/php5/bin/php-config
    ```

5. Run make and make install.

    ```
    [Blossom:/usr/local/src/xdebug] make
    [Blossom:/usr/local/src/xdebug] make install
    ```

6. Copy the modules to your PHP extensions directory. The make and make install process will create a modules directory with the XDebug module. Copy this into your PHP extensions directory, the same one that you put dbg.so in earlier.

    ```
    [Blossom:/usr/local/src/xdebug]cp modules/xdebug.so
    /path/to/php_extensions_directory
    ```

You now have a compiled XDebug binary installed. You must now configure your `php.ini` file to use the XDebug.

Configure php.ini

These instructions assume that you have gone through the `php.ini` configuration earlier to use DBG. If not, follow the steps to turn on `implicit_flush` and to deactivate eAccelerator. Remember, also, if you are using XAMPP, you will need to edit three copies of `php.ini` if you intend to switch back and forth between PHP4 and PHP5.

1. Deactivate the DBG directives since DBG and XDebug will conflict with each other. Deactivate the DBG directives by commenting them out of `php.ini`.

   ```
   ;extension=php_Dbg.dll
   [debugger]
   ;debugger.enabled = true
   ;debugger.profiler_enabled = true
   ;debugger.JIT_host = clienthost
   ;debugger.JIT_port = 7869
   ```

2. Add the XDebug directive. We need to tell PHP to load the XDebug module. Do this by adding the following line to `php.ini`:

   `zend_extension="`*/path_to/*`xdebug.so"`

Do not forget the quotation marks. If you wish to switch back to DBG in the future, comment this line out and re-enable the DBG directives.

Save your changes and restart Apache. This will enable the XDebug module. Reload your original `phpinfo()` page, and your copyright notice should now display XDebug instead of DBG.

This program makes use of the Zend Scripting Language Engine:
Zend Engine v2.0.4-dev, Copyright (c) 1998-2004 Zend Technologies
with Xdebug v2.0.0beta2, Copyright (c) 2002, 2003, 2004, by Derick Rethans

Powered By

Now that we have XDebug loaded, we can go ahead and start using XDebug in debugging our modules.

XDebug module keeps its preferences in its own settings. We will need to go into these settings and specify the location of the PHP interpreter before we start creating configuration profiles. To access these settings, go to the Windows | Preferences... | PHPEclipse Web Development | PHP | XDebug menu option.

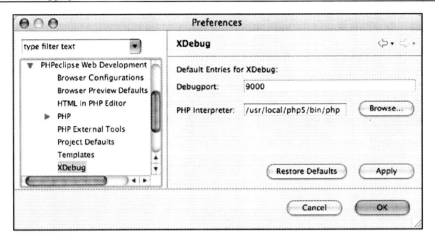

PHPEclipse will attempt to connect to XDebug throught the port specified in the Debugport field. By default, XDebug will use this port, and thus, PHPEclipse will also try to use this port. If you change the connection port in php.ini, you will also need to change it in here.

The PHP Interpreter field is important. This will specify the default PHP binary that PHPEclipse will try to use. Click on the Browse... button and specify the active PHP binary. After both fields are filled, click on the OK button to store the settings. We can now create an XDebug debugger profile.

An XDebug debugger profile works the same way as a DBG debugger profile. We are going to create a profile for each script that we want to debug. We will enter settings in each profile that tell Eclipse which file we are debugging and where to find critical project and PHP information. The only difference is the screens themselves.

We are going to create a debugging profile for the debug.php file that we've been using. In that file, set a couple of breakpoints. Right-click on the left margin and select 'Toggle Breakpoint'. You may see an option for 'Toggle PHP Breakpoint', but this is not the option that we need.

Go to the XDebug profile creation screen by selecting the Run menu | Debug... | PHP XDebug Script. Click on the New button to create a new profile. This will create a local debugging profile.

In the future, remote debugging will probably be supported. Create a new configuration under PHP XDebug Remote Script to create a remote configuration. However, as of this writing, remote debugging is incomplete and not supported.

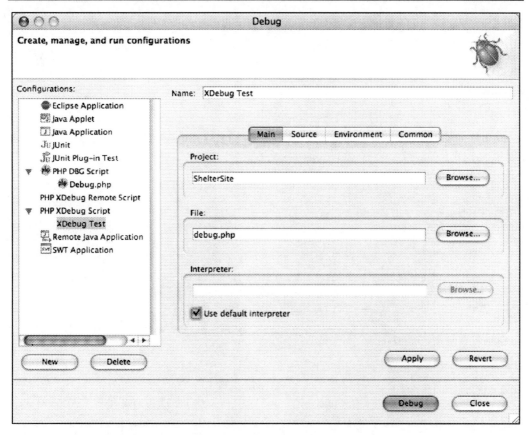

Give a name for this profile in the Name field. The Project field is filled in automatically based on the project context where you've created this profile. In the File field, click on the Browse... button to select the file that you wish to debug. Select the debug.php file that we've created.

As long as you have specified a default interpreter, you can leave the Use default interpreter checkbox checked. Click on the Apply button to save your changes.

Currently, the Source and Common tabs are not used. However, we will need to set a dummy environment variable. Click on the Environment tab to set this variable:

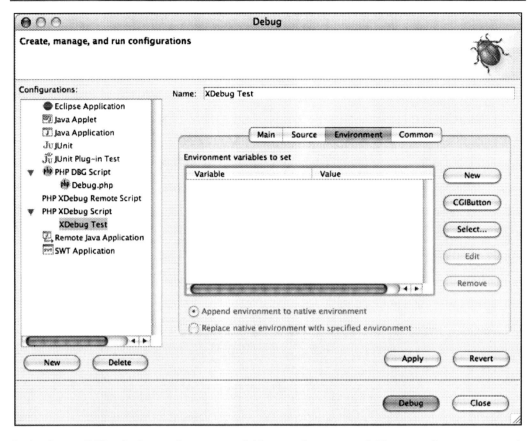

In the future, CGI and other environment variables may be supported. However, for now, we need to add an environment variable to trigger the debugger client. Click on the New button to create a new environment variable:

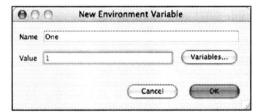

Enter a variable name and a value in the New Environment Variable dialog box and then click OK. It does not matter what the value or name is. For current versions of PHPeclipse, we need to do this to trigger the client to report all variables.

Once you are finished, click the Debug button. This will execute the debugging process. The debugger should stop at the first breakpoint. The variables and breakpoints will work the same way as for the DBG debugging module:

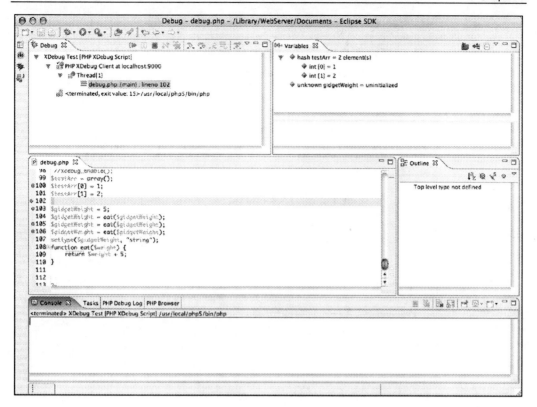

Summary

The debugger is an important and valuable toolset of PHPEclipse and any IDE. Using it, we can pause and continue the execution of our program at any line. While it's stopped, we can examine variables to verify that they're holding the right values and change them to do further testing. Without an IDE, we'd have to check variables by echoing them out onto the web page. This causes us to alter our application with code that does not have anything to do with the required functionality.

Currently, the PHPEclipse debugger lacks a few features that the Eclipse debugger for Java has. For example, PHPEclipse is missing:

- Conditional breakpoints: The ability to stop the debugger when a certain condition is met. For example, stopping the debugger when a variable changes values.

- Breakpoint hit counts: The ability to stop the debugger when a breakpoint has been reached a certain number of times. This is very helpful for loops.

However, debugging is one of the most active development areas of PHPEclipse. We have already experimented with new features such as XDebug support and variable watching. As more work is done on PHPEclipse, we will certainly see more features that will bring the PHP debugger parity with the JDT debugger.

6
Using the Quantum DB Plug-In

One of the most important innovations that helped mature the Internet was the use of database-driven websites. The concept is rather simple—store data in a database and use this data to build web pages. Changing stored data is quicker than changing and publishing a static web page. Stored data can also be updated through other means, many automated, whereas a web development team would have to manually manage a static site's changes. On the other end, databases allow users to interact with the site by creating applications that directly interface with the database. E-commerce sites, discussion forums, and auction sites are just three examples. Database-driven websites reduce maintenance effort while dramatically increasing what we can do online.

Today, database-driven sites are ubiquitous. Web scripting languages bridged the gap between stored data in a repository and its presentation on the web server. Almost all programming languages, including PHP, have components to query and to manipulate databases. In order to be effective, web developers must be able to use databases effectively and efficiently.

It isn't enough for web developers to master only the database connectivity functionality of their programming language. A good web developer needs to have a solid understanding of **Structured Query Language (SQL)**, the *lingua franca* of database access. In the process of development, a web developer will need to query the database outside of the application. Common reasons include:

- Examining the schema of a database
- Testing SQL statements
- Inserting, changing, or deleting test data
- On solo projects, changing the schema of the database

Developers often need to switch over to a database client tool to query the external database, for example, a terminal for command-line clients or a GUI client tool. PHPEclipse helps us by including the Quantum DB plug-in to work with databases. The Quantum DB plug-in turns Eclipse into a database client. With the Quantum DB view, we can interact with our database and see the results without having to exit Eclipse.

In this chapter, we will explore the Quantum DB plug-in. We will first take a brief look at relational databases and SQL, see how to connect to a database from Eclipse, and experiment on that database using Quantum DB.

Relational Databases

A vast majority of modern databases are still **relational databases**. The entire database system is referred to as a relational database management system (RDBMS). RDBMSs group related data into table structures. Each stored record is a row in the table. Columns in the table define what is stored in each table. A column has strict rules that lay down what is allowed in each row's entry for that column. For example, some columns only allow integers, and some must be filled with a value while some can be left blank. The 'relational' part of a RDBMS comes from the relationships between the tables. Tables can, and usually do, have keys. Each key is a unique identifier for the record in a table. This can be as complex as multiple columns designated as a key, or as simple as a column holding a unique number. Keys can be referenced in other tables. These references make up relationships.

SQL (pronounced 'es-que-el') is the standard language used to interact with the database. SQL allows you to navigate the relationships between tables to grab exactly what you want from the database. The SQL language is divided into two parts—the functionality that allows you to manipulate data and the functionality that allows you to change the database and table structures. In corporate environments, permission for the latter is often reserved for database administrators.

IBM developed SQL in the early days of relational databases. Today, the American National Standards Institute (ANSI) is the steward of the SQL language. However, database vendors often add their own extensions to the SQL language, and sometimes even change the behavior of standard SQL keywords.

The 'system' part of RDBMS roughly defines the server component of the database. The vast majority of modern RDBMSs are servers. The way you interact with the database is through a client and often, an RDBMS ships with its own client. These clients give native commands to the server to interact with data or change the structure of the database. Clients can take the form of a simple command-line application in which you type SQL or they could be a GUI application. RDBMSs can also take third-party clients. For example, the popular open source RDBMS, MySQL, includes a command-line client. However, the open source community has developed numerous GUI clients for MySQL. A client can even be an Eclipse plug-in, which is what the Quantum DB plug-in is.

JDBC

In order to support third-party clients, databases need a separate layer to translate commands into the RDBMS's native commands. Think of it as a translator between clients and the database. In the mid 90's, Microsoft developed an **API (Application Programming Interface)** to interact RDBMSs with different clients. This API is called **Open Database Connectivity (ODBC)**. Among other features, ODBC translates SQL statements into native database commands. Each RDBMS vendor is responsible for creating the ODBC driver for its product.

ODBC is written in C. This made it natively inaccessible to Java. To work around this, Sun created **Java Database Connectivity (JDBC)** API. In simplest terms, JDBC does what ODBC does, but in Java. Some key advantages that JDBC has over ODBC are that JDBC is a native Java solution, and it offers functionalities not available in ODBC. Like ODBC, in order to connect to a database using JDBC, the RDBMS vendor must develop a JDBC driver for its system.

Sun also includes a **JDBC-ODBC Bridge** in the JDBC API for RDBMSs that do not support JDBC, but support ODBC. You may also run across such terms as 'type IV driver'. Types I-IV refer to the level of 'pure Javaness' of the driver, with IV being 100% Java. Ideally, you'll want a type IV driver. These days, since Java is so prevalent in business environments, most RDBMSs offer a type IV JDBC driver.

The Quantum DB Plug-In

The Quantum DB plug-in is an open source RDBMS plug-in for Eclipse. The Quantum DB project is hosted on SourceForge at `http://quantum.sourceforge.net/`. This plug-in is included as part of the PHPEclipse package. You may want to check out the project site for new Quantum DB releases, since the version we have came bundled with our release version of PHPEclipse and an improved version of Quantum DB might be available.

Quantum DB uses JDBC and this allows Eclipse to become a GUI database client. Using Quantum DB's views, you can execute SQL commands and view the results directly in Eclipse. Using the GUI tools and shortcuts, you can even do everything you need to a database without writing a single line of SQL code.

Setting Up the Environment

In order to use the Quantum DB plug-in, we will need three components:

- A relational database system: We need a database to store the data that powers our site.

- A JDBC driver: We will need to download and install the JDBC driver to allow the Quantum DB plug-in to talk to our database.

- Eclipse/Quantum DB plug-in: Finally, we need the client piece itself. However, we won't need to install anything special at this point. The Quantum DB plug-in was installed when you installed PHPEclipse.

The Development Database

Up to this point, the book examples have been assuming that you are running MySQL on your local workstation. We will continue to use this configuration in our examples. If you need to install MySQL, there are several easy ways to do this. First off, if you are using XAMPP, a MySQL installation is included as part of the XAMPP package. Simply start the MySQL database server from the XAMPP control panel. If you are using Linux or Mac OS X, the installation process is simple. Go to the official MySQL download site at `http://www.mysql.com/` and download an appropriate binary installer for your system. Regardless of which method you choose, be aware that you should secure the initial system by setting a root password. The MySQL manual's section on post-installation configuration at `http://dev.mysql.com/doc/refman/5.1/en/default-privileges.html` describes this process.

If you have a development database somewhere, you can certainly connect to it and follow along. Since JDBC is an abstracted layer, all we really need to know about our database is where it is and which RDBMS it is.

Other JDBC Drivers

Here are links to JDBC drivers for other popular database systems:

PostgreSQL: `http://jdbc.postgresql.org/`

Oracle: `http://www.oracle.com/technology/software/tech/java/sqlj_jdbc/`

Microsoft SQL Server: `http://www.microsoft.com/sql/downloads/2005/jdbc.mspx`

Sybase: `http://www.sybase.com/products/informationmanagement/softwaredeveloperkit/jconnect`

For Microsoft SQL Server and Sybase, you may want to consider using the jTDS JDBC driver. jTDS is an open source project that provides a free JDBC driver for SQL Server and Sybase. Why would you want to use jTDS when the commercial versions are available? Support and cost are two reasons. jTDS has an active support community while vendor drivers may require a support contract. You can learn more about jTDS at the official project page at `http://jtds.sourceforge.net/`. For other databases, check with your manufacturer for available JDBC drivers.

Downloading and Installing the MySQL JDBC Driver

The MySQL JDBC driver is called MySQL Connector/J. You can find this software under Downloads in the MySQL Connectors section of the MySQL website. MySQL usually will have two or three version numbers available, the immediate past release, a recommended and production-ready version, and a development version. For stability reasons, you should download the recommended version. Since JDBC drivers are written in Java, one binary will work on all platforms.

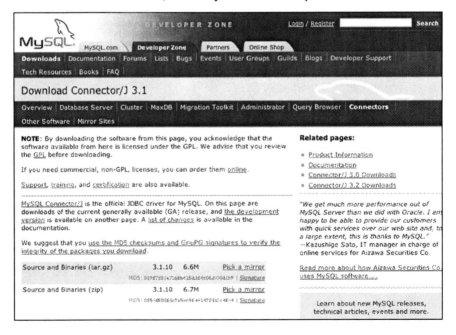

After you download the package, uncompress it. Inside, you'll find documentation on using JDBC from within Java and the driver itself. The drivers are JAR files. The MySQL package comes with two connectors—a regular connector and one compiled with debugging options (the –g flag). Either one will work.

Now, we should move the connector to an appropriate place. Theoretically, you could place the connector anywhere. However, we should treat these as standard Java JARs. If you are doing Java development, or plan to, you will definitely need to move the connector to a place that the JVM can access. You have two options for this.

The simplest way is to install it in your JAVA_HOME external libraries. The standard Java installation has a special directory for third-party libraries. You can place it in there. This is located at $JAVA_HOME/jre/lib/ext (for example, C:\j2sdk1.4.2_05\jre\lib\ext). In Mac OS X, the jre directory is integrated. The directory will be /System/Library/Frameworks/ JavaVM.framework/Home/lib/ext. Note that Home is an alias to a location further down in the directory structure. The drawback to installing it under JAVA_HOME is that you will need to move the libraries whenever you upgrade Java on your workstation.

To make the libraries Java-version independent, you can install them in your CLASSPATH environment variable. The JVM looks for libraries in your CLASSPATH environment variable when it compiles. The drawback to this is that it involves a few more steps, and can vary wildly if you are not using a Windows machine. First, define a location that you wish to use and move the connector there. Then, in Windows, go to your Start | Settings | Control Panel | System | Advanced | Environment Variables. Click on the New button under User variables. Type CLASSPATH for the Variable name and the full path to the connector for the Variable value. Click the OK button.

In Mac OS X, type this in the command line:

```
[Blossom:~] shuchow% setenv CLASSPATH '/path/to/mysql-connector-java-3.1.10-bin-
g.jar'
```

Note that the directory path is a full path to the connector JAR itself. This will create the CLASSPATH variable for your session. If you want it to last longer than just the time your machine is up and running, edit your login file. It is a hidden file named .login located in your user directory. Add this code to the end of the .login file:

```
set CLASSPATH = '/path/to/mysql-connector-java-3.1.10-bin-g.jar'
```

This method will also work for **bsh**-compatible shells under Linux. Whichever location you choose, remember where you've installed it. We will need to point to this driver later on.

Using the Quantum DB Plug-In

We can now start using Eclipse to connect to our database. Most of our work will be done in the Quantum DB perspective. Open this perspective by choosing the Window | Open Perspective... | Other... | Quantum DB menu option.

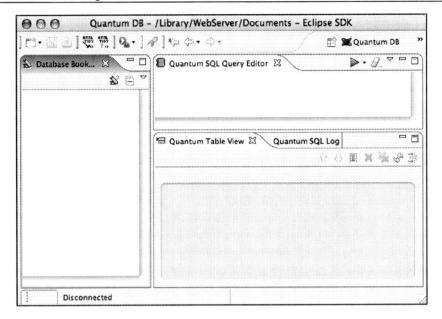

The perspective is made up of five views:

- The Database Bookmarks view manages the links to databases. In order to use a database, you must create a bookmark to it.

- Quantum SQL Query Editor accepts SQL statements. Type and run your SQL statements in here and Eclipse will send it to the active database connection.

- The results of the query are displayed in the Quantum Table View.

- The Quantum SQL Log shows all the SQL commands sent by Eclipse, and the success or error message.

- The JDBC Driver view shows information about the JDBC drivers loaded. Unfortunately, you do not use this view to manage the drivers. It only shows what drivers you have installed. This view is not seen in the perspective by default. You will have to open it by going to the Window | Show View | Other... | QuantumDB | JDBC Driver View menu option.

Before we can start writing queries and browsing through a database, we need to set up Eclipse to use the database. Once we get the driver loaded and the database identified, we can go ahead and start using the Quantum DB to interact with our database.

Setting Up a Database in Quantum DB

This initial setup involves telling Eclipse that a JDBC driver is present, and then using the driver to point to a database. These two requirements can take place in a series of seamless steps.

First, in the Bookmarks view, click on the New Bookmark icon (💸). You can also right-click on the view and select New Bookmark. This will bring up a wizard to guide you along:

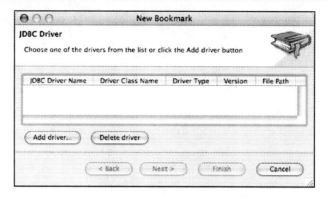

To add or delete new databases to drivers, you need to go back to this wizard by clicking the New Bookmark icon from the Database Bookmarks view. You can then manage the drivers from here. If you wish to delete a driver, highlight it here and click Delete driver.

For now, click on the Add driver... button to select the JDBC driver on your workstation:

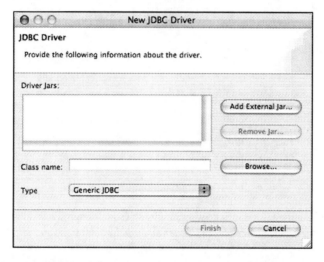

At first the Driver Jars box will be empty. As you add more JDBC drivers, they will appear in this box. Click on Add External Jar... and select the driver connector JAR file from your file system to add the driver. JDBC driver JARs can also be removed from this window.

MySQL uses just one JAR file as the driver. Some other database vendors use more than one file to make up the connector. If the JDBC driver you downloaded has more than one file, add all of them here.

Next, you need to select the class name of the driver; click on the Browse...button to see all of the classes available in the installed driver JARs. Eclipse grabs all of the classes associated with the installed JARs and lets you pick from them.

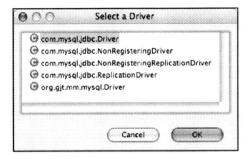

Select com.mysql.jdbc.Driver. This is the main JDBC driver in the JAR file. Click on the OK button.

This will dismiss the window and bring you back to the list of installed JARs.

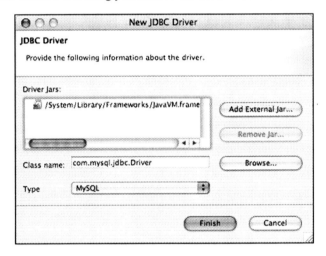

The Class name field will now be filled with the class you selected. To finish this step, select MySQL from the Type pull-down menu. You can also see the wide variety of databases supported by Quantum DB in this pull-down menu. Click on the Finish button.

This will bring you back to the New Bookmark window. At this point, the driver has been specified. You can go back to the main Eclipse screen and see the driver in the JDBC Driver view. However, we need to finish adding our database as a bookmark before we can use it.

If you dropped out of the bookmark adding process to see the JDBC Driver view, you can get back to the New Bookmark window by clicking on the New Bookmark icon in the Database Bookmarks view. Remember, the JDBC Driver view only gives you information on which drivers are installed. It does not let you manage the drivers. As of version 2.4.5 of the Quantum DB plug-in, you'll need to use the New Bookmark icon to add database bookmarks to drivers. In other words, if you want to connect to another MySQL database, regardless of whether it's on your local machine or on another server, you'll need to get back to this window using the New Bookmark icon.

The driver that you just added can be seen in this window. From the New Bookmark window, select the newly added driver and click the Next button. This will bring you to the Connection details window:

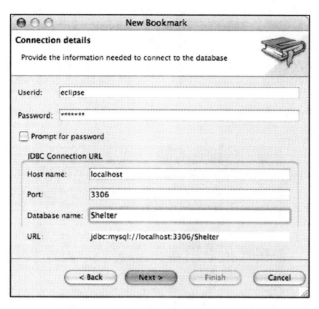

Here, you add user name, password, and server information for your database. We use the user name and password that we defined earlier. Since our example is running locally, we are using localhost as the Host name. The name of the database that we set up is Shelter. The URL is a dynamically created JDBC connection string. If you have used JDBC in Java development, you'll know that a special connection string is used to tell the Connection Manager the details of your connection. This step in the Quantum DB wizard automatically creates the string and uses Eclipse to pass the connection information on to the JVM.

If you are using a remote development database, add the appropriate information to this screen. If you work in an environment with a database administrator on staff, you can get this connection information from them.

Click on the Next button to continue. You will get a window prompting you for a name for the bookmark you just created:

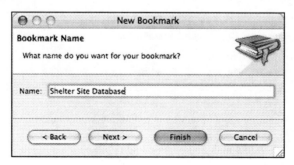

Give your bookmark a name on this window. At this point, that is all you need to start using the shelter database with the Quantum DB plug-in. Click on the Finish button to stop the wizard. If you have a database that supports schemas, most notably DB2 and Oracle, clicking the Next button would allow you to specify which schema you would like to open by default.

Using a Database in Quantum DB

Your database bookmark is now ready to be used. We can immediately see some of the features of the plug-in from the Database Bookmarks view. Your new database bookmark will appear in the Database Bookmarks view. Double-click on this to connect to the database. This will connect Eclipse to the database using the connection settings you specified in the wizard. The plug-in will query the database for the entire schema and represent it in a hierarchical form.

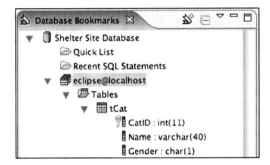

The first thing that you'll notice is that the bookmark icon by the bookmark name has turned into a database icon ( ). This means that there is an active connection to the database.

The Quick List folder will appear for all databases. You can store tables in here as a shortcut. The Recent SQL Statements folder holds the most recent SQL statements that you entered into the Quantum SQL Query Editor.

Finally, we see the database schema itself. This is represented by the 'user name @ database server' format. Clicking on the expand/collapse icon will expand to show the items in the database. The items are organized as views, tables, and stored procedures. Since we're using a simple MySQL database, we see the one table, tCat, that's listed under the Tables folder and an empty Views folder. If we expand the tCat table, we see the names of columns of the database along with their data types. You will see a 'key' icon next to the name if the column is a key.

There are only two toolbar icons and a Menu icon for the Database Bookmarks view.

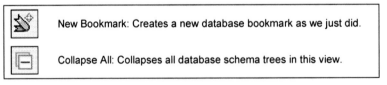

The Menu icon in this view holds several useful information-related options.

- Show Table Sizes will put the number of rows that a table has beside its table name.
- Show Database Info will put the vendor and version of the database beside the bookmark name.
- Import/Export Bookmarks will export information about the database bookmarks into an XML file. This allows you to share information about your databases with other team members.

Writing SQL Statements

To send SQL statements to your database, use the Quantum SQL Query Editor view. Write statements as if you were using a command-line client. After you are finished, click on the Execute icon (▶ ▾).

In this example, we enter a simple SELECT * FROM tCat in the view and then click on the Execute icon:

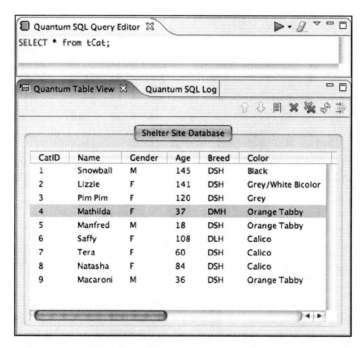

This statement will pull all records and columns from the tCat table of our database. The results from this statement are shown in the Quantum Table View. This view only shows record sets from SELECT statements. If your statement does not return a record set, for example, if it is an UPDATE, INSERT, or DELETE statement, the Quantum Table View will not be updated.

The Query Editor can take multiple SQL commands. If you have entered more than one command, you simply select the ones you want to execute in the Query Editor. If you select a portion of all the commands and click the Execute button (this icon will now read as Execute against "Shelter Site Database"), only the highlighted statements or portions of the statements will execute.

If you have multiple SELECT statements, each result set will appear as its own tab under the Quantum Table View. To see what happens, enter the following three statements into the Query Editor. However, highlight only the last two before you hit the Execute button.

```
SELECT Name from tCat;
SELECT Gender from tCat;
SELECT Age from tCat;
```

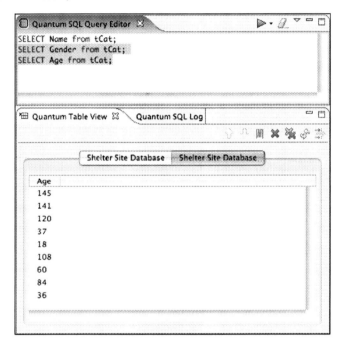

You will get two new tabs in the Quantum Table View, signifying that only the last two statements were executed.

Every command you enter into the editor gets stored in the Recent SQL Searches folder in the Database Bookmarks view. To use statements from this folder you simply need to double-click the statement. It will populate itself in the Quantum SQL Query Editor view. Click on Execute in the toolbar to run this query. By default, twenty recent statements are saved. You can change this number in the Window | Preferences | Quantum DB menu option. Enter the number of results you want saved in Maximum Size of Query History.

There are two toolbar buttons and a pull-down menu in the Quantum SQL Query Editor.

Execute: Executes the SQL statement highlighted in the editor, or the entire contents of the SQL editor if nothing is highlighted. Execute also has a pull-down menu. All your database bookmarks will appear here. If you have more than one database bookmark, you can select the bookmark to execute the statement against through this pull-down menu.

 Clear: Clears the entire SQL editor.

The pull-down menu allows you to export and import queries from text files. If your database supports rollbacks and commits, you can give those commands in their respective options in this pull-down menu. MySQL simply auto-commits when commands are given, so this option is automatically checked in the pull-down menu.

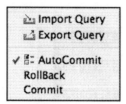

Working with the Quantum Table View Result Sets

There are several tools in the Quantum Table View that will be helpful to you, as well as overcome some quirks in how record sets are displayed.

By default, only 200 rows are shown at a time when you execute a SELECT statement against a database. The first three icons in the toolbar are used to address this. The other icons address the data shown in this view.

 Previous: Takes you to the previous set of 200 rows in the result set.

 Next: Takes you to the next set of 200 rows in the result set.

 Toggle Show All Table Rows: Shows all of the records returned in the statement, thereby making Previous and Next useless for this result set.

 Close Result Set: Closes the result set that you currently have focused.

 Close All Result Sets: Deletes all result sets in the view.

 Refresh: Refreshes the data from the database.

 Filter and Sort: Allows you to filter and sort the result set.

Filter and Sort deserve some special attention. If you have ever worked with a Microsoft Access database, you will know how easily the GUI tools there allow you to write queries without writing any SQL code. The Quantum Table View's Filter and Sort function works in similar fashion.

To use the Filter and Sort functions, you'll need to double-click on the tCat table directly from the Database Bookmarks view. You can also right-click on the table name and select View Table from the contextual menu. Both of these options are equivalent to a SELECT * statement. The Table View will populate with the results from the query. Be aware that to use Filter and Sort, you need to populate the Table View by either one of the aforementioned methods—double-clicking on the table or selecting View Table from the table's contextual menu. You cannot simply write a SELECT statement in the SQL editor and then use Filter and Sort, even though the same result set will be in the Table View. Once you have the result set up, click on the Filter and Sort icon. You will get this screen:

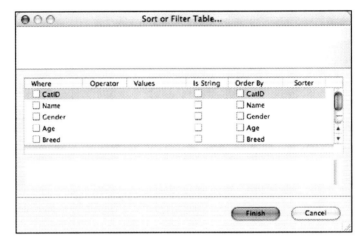

This wizard dynamically creates a WHERE clause for your SELECT statement. You set the values shown below to create your WHERE clause:

- Where is the column criteria that you wish to specify.

- Operator allows you to test if the criteria are equal to (=), not equal to (<>), less than (<), or greater than (>). Click on this column, in the row you wish to test, for a pull-down menu of all the available operators.

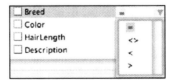

- Values are the criteria to test. This is a freeform textbox where you enter the value you want to test.

- If the value is a string, check the checkbox in the Is String column. This will add single quotes to the Values you specify. Otherwise, the filter assumes that the column is an integer and thus, does not require quotation marks.
- You can also specify an Order By clause for the query.
- Sorter allows you to select if the Order By is to be ascending or descending.

For example, let's create a filter that selects only the domestic short hair (DSH) cats from the tCat table. We'll need to create a filter for all cats where Breed is equal to the string DSH. We'll also order the results returned by CatID in ascending order.

1. Check Breed in the Where column.
2. Select the = operator from the Operator pull-down menu.
3. Type DSH, without quotation marks, in the Values column.
4. Check the Is String checkbox. The value will be enclosed in single quotes when this box is checked. You will need to click this checkbox for any column that is a string. Otherwise, MySQL will throw an error since it will treat values without quotes as integers even when the datatype might be a string based type like a varchar.
5. We'll order by the CatID, so check the checkbox next to CatID in the Order By column.
6. Select ASC in the Sorter pulldown of the CatID row to do an ascending search on CatID.

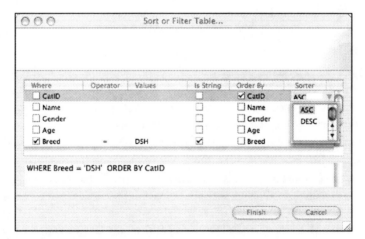

7. Click on the Finish button.

The WHERE clause that you dynamically create will appear at the bottom of the dialog box. Once you click on the Finish button, the tCat result set will update itself as per this WHERE clause.

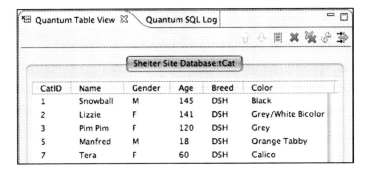

To clear the filter, click on the Filter and Sort icon again. The filter criteria will be blank (nothing checked). With no criteria, just click on the Finish button to clear the filter. Alternatively, you can enter in new criteria to do a new filter of the result set.

> If you use SQL a lot in your web development, you will find the Quantum SQL Query Editor and Quantum Table View to be the most important views in the Quantum DB plug-in. You may want to add these two views to the PHPEclipse perspective. That way, you do not have to leave your PHP code to enter SQL queries and view their results. This is just another way that lets you customize the Eclipse IDE to your specific needs.

Quantum DB Shortcuts

In the Database Bookmarks, right-click on the tCat table to see some helpful shortcuts in the contextual menu:

- View Table will execute a SELECT * on the table. The results will appear in the Quantum Table View.

- Delete All Rows will delete all rows in the table. Eclipse will ask you to confirm if you really want to do that before executing this function.

- View Table Details will query the database for the schema. In MySQL, this is the same as EXPLAIN tCat.

- Add to Quick List will add the entity to your Quick List folder. This folder is helpful if you have a database with many tables, views, and stored procedures. By defining Quick List items, you can isolate particular items you are working with at that time.

- Remove from Quick List will remove an item from the Quick List if it has been quick listed.

In the SQL Statements menu, there is an option called Drop Table/View/Sequence... This option will take you to a wizard that dynamically generates a DROP statement for you:

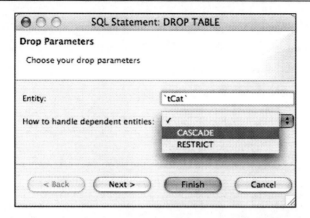

Enter the name of the table you want to DROP in the Entity option. How to handle dependent entities asks you how you wish to handle foreign key constraints. This is dependent on whether your database supports cascading and restricting when deleting a table with foreign key constraints.

You can click on the Finish button to execute the DROP. You can also click on the Next button to view and verify that the SQL statement generated by Eclipse is correct, and you are not accidentally destroying any data you do not wish to be deleted.

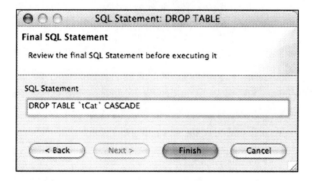

Click on the Finish button to execute the drop.

Back in the table contextual menu, there is a Properties option. Click on this to view the properties not only for the table, but for the database in general. This is a view-only screen. The parameters in this window cannot be changed.

There is also an option for Custom Copy with three slots. To set it up, go to the Window | Preferences | Quantum DB | Copy menu option. Select one of the Custom Copy templates available. Custom Copy is a helpful, but often overlooked and complex automation tool from the Quantum DB plug-in. Custom Copy automatically pastes text into your clipboard depending on the tables and columns you highlight in the Database Bookmarks view.

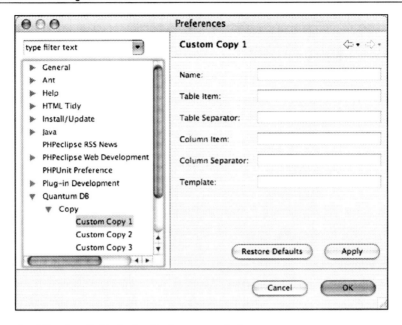

You will see the following fields in the Preferences window:

- **Name** is the name of this Custom Copy template. Give it a descriptive name.
- **Table Item** is what you want to be copied for each table encountered.
- **Table Separator** is the string that separates each Table Item.
- **Column Item** is what you want to be copied for each column encountered.
- **Column Separator** is the string that separates each Column Item.
- **Template** is what you want to paste to your clipboard.

These entries can take the following variables:

- `${schema}`: The schema of the table or column. Valid in all format fields except Template. Again, since schemas are not supported in MySQL, we will ignore this variable.
- `${table}`: The table name, without schema. Valid in all format fields except Template.
- `${qualified}`: Same as `${schema}` and `${table}` concatenated together. Valid in all format fields except Template.
- `${column}`: The column name. Only valid for the Column Item field.
- `${column_list}`: The list of all columns. Only valid for the Table Item field.
- `${table_list}`: The list of all tables. Only valid in Template. This is the only variable that can be used in Template.
- `\n`: Inserts a new line.
- `\t`: Inserts a tab character.

The key to this tool is to remember the following:

- For every column you highlight in the Database Bookmarks view, whatever you enter in the Column Item fields will get copied to the clipboard.

- The column items make up the ${column_list} variable.

- For every table you highlight in the Database Bookmarks view, whatever you enter in the Table Item fields will get copied to the clipboard.

- For every table you highlight in the Database Bookmarks view, the copy aggregator will implicitly hit each column. The column items will be collected and aggregated into the ${column_list} variable.

- The table items make up the ${table_list} variable.

- You must enter the ${table_list} variable in the Template field, otherwise, the Custom Copy function will not copy anything dynamic to the clipboard.

Let's take a look at an example on how we can use this tool.

Suppose there is a rule in your company that you cannot use SELECT * in your code. You must explicitly name all column names in SELECT statements. If your table is small, this shouldn't be a big problem. However, if the table is large, it can be a hassle to manually type all the column names into your IDE. A lot of GUI tools do not have the mechanism to grab just the column names. Even if you use a command line to get the database schema, you often have to delete extraneous information like data types. The Custom Copy feature can make this simple for you.

Go into the Custom Copy Preferences and select the first template. Enter the following values:

- For the Name field, enter Name Columns.
  This is simply the name that we're giving this template.

- For the Table Item field, enter 'SELECT ${column_list} FROM ${table}'.
  Every time a table is encountered from the highlighted list in Database Bookmarks view, it will copy this to the clipboard. The ${table} variable will be substituted with the name of the current table.

- For the Table Separator field, enter '\n'.
  This will place a new line after each SELECT statement.

- For the Column Item field, enter '${column}'.
  This will take the name of the column and substitute it whenever a column is encountered. Remember, the columns of the table are implicitly traversed whenever you have a table highlighted, and collectively, they make up the ${column_list}, which is specific to each table.

- For the Column Separator, enter ', '.
  This will put a comma and space in between each column name in the column list.

- For the Template field, enter '${table_list}'.
  Collectively, table items make up the ${table_list}. This is the final step for dynamic creation of a table.

Now, select the tcat table from the **Database Bookmarks** view. Highlight the table name and right-click. Select **Custom Copy | Name Columns**. The values you entered will be copied into the database, with the tcat table as the input. Now, paste into any text editor and you should see the following code:

```
SELECT CatID, Name, Gender, Age, Breed FROM tCat
```

If you wish to see this in action on a more complex database, you can make a database bookmark to the MySQL administration table in a local MySQL installation. Click on several tables and you will see SELECT statements generated automatically:

```
SELECT Host, Db, Select_priv, Insert_priv, Update_priv, Delete_priv,
Create_priv, Drop_priv, Grant_priv, References_priv, Index_priv, Alter_priv,
Create_tmp_table_priv, Lock_tables_priv FROM host
SELECT name,ret,dl,type FROM func
SELECT Host, Db, User, Select_priv, Insert_priv, Update_priv, Delete_priv,
Create_priv, Drop_priv, Grant_priv, References_priv, Index_priv, Alter_priv,
Create_tmp_table_priv, Lock_tables_priv FROM db
SELECT Host, Db, User, Table_name, Column_name, Timestamp, Column_priv FROM
columns_priv
```

Custom Copy is not very self-explanatory and the official documentation is a bit poor. However, once understood, it can be very helpful in writing scripts that center around your database schema.

Summary

The Quantum DB plug-in demonstrates yet again the flexibility of Eclipse. With it, Eclipse becomes a full-featured database client. The setup involves installing a JDBC driver and pointing the driver to the database that we need. From there, we can write SQL queries and view the results in Eclipse using the Quantum DB perspective.

If writing SQL statements is not your strength, Quantum DB offers shortcuts that allow us to query tables, write filters, and view schema and database information.

7

Version Control

The question of how to manage your source code will inevitably come up while working on any project. A lot of times, using a simple file server would be enough. However, using formal version control software has many benefits. In this chapter, we'll explore some of those benefits and see how to leverage them using Eclipse and two popular version control systems—**CVS** and **Subversion**.

First, let us address a small issue with terminology. You'll encounter many generic terms that describe a software package that stores and keeps track of source code—version tracking system, versioning software, version control system, control versioning system, etc. Since the letters often include C, V, and S, the acronym CVS is often used to refer to a generic software package. However, CVS is one of the most popular versioning systems. Its acronym stands for **Concurrent Versioning System**. People sometimes use these terms interchangeably, but there is a distinct difference between the generic package and the formal product.

Version Control Overview

In its most basic form, version control is a place to maintain source code files. There is a server component, where the files are stored, and a client component that retrieves and places files into a server. The key benefits and differences over a simple file server include:

- **Work share**: In some form, the versioning software should have tools to let team members know who is working on what. Often, this is a locking mechanism that gives one user 'exclusive' rights to a file, but tells other people on the team, 'Hey, Joe is working on that file'.

- **Historical preservation**: Control versioning software must store a file's history of changes and should be able to restore any prior version if necessary. Even if you are a lone web developer not in a team, this feature alone makes versioning systems worth using. If you need to research the exact state of a source file six months ago, this software can retrieve that file for you.

- **Backup**: By having an entire copy of your application, you have a backup stored on another server in case something happens to your workspace hard drive.

- **Maintain versions of an application**: Most versioning applications make it easy for you to keep track of different versions of an application, and eventually, to merge them back into one application. For example, you can work on adding new features without disturbing the original code base that is in production.

- **Workflow automation**: Versioning software can keep labels and flags on each source code file. Using these flags, you can automate the process of pushing files to a development, acceptance, or production server using scripts. For example, if a bug fix involves three different files in three different directories, you can tag the files in the repository with a label. When it's time to move the files to an acceptance server for testing, a script can simply search the repository for tagged files and move them out automatically. Three files might still be manageable, but when you're adding a new feature involving fifty files across different directories and another team member is working in those directories, this feature can save a lot of confusion.

- **Security**: Versioning software keeps files in a different area. Often this is a completely different server than public network shares, where everyone in a company has access rights. This gives you finer control on who has what access to the source code.

Terms and Concepts

The world of version control, and CVS and Subversion in particular, has its own terminology and metaphors. These terms are frequently found in everything from installation to usage. Before we can work with CVS or Subversion, let's take a brief tour of the different terms we will encounter.

The server stores all your source code in a special place in the file system called a **repository**. The repository is really just a mirror of your source tree with some additional special metadata files needed by the server. In CVS, the repository directory is also referred to as the **cvsroot** directory. In CVS, these metafiles are stored in a directory named CVSROOT, which is not to be confused with the cvsroot directory itself! Each application that is stored and controlled in the server gets its own directory under cvsroot. As in Eclipse, applications are called **projects**.

You also have a place where you actually work on and edit your source code. This location is called the **sandbox**, and should include a complete copy of the application that is stored in the versioning server.

You may have noticed the relationship between the workspace location, document root, and now the sandbox. By converging on these three locations, we certainly make it a lot easier for web development. With just one location, we can grab work files, edit them, and preview them in our web serving environment. This eliminates the need to shuffle files around from different directories.

Branching is the idea of splitting off a copy of your source code into another area, so that we can work adding new features on the new copy. Using a tree metaphor, this split-off copy is called the **branch**. Meanwhile, the original copy, referred to as the **trunk** or **Head**, still exists for you to do maintenance work. Common wisdom dictates that the code in Head should be the version in production, or very close to it. When you are ready, the new features of the branch are re-integrated back with the maintained code. This is called '**merging** back into the trunk'.

As you may have guessed by now, Eclipse includes hooks into version tracking software. The Eclipse interface doesn't directly give you all these benefits. For example, if you want scripts to automatically deploy files, you'll have to write them yourself. However, the process of moving files in and out of the control versioning software's repository system can be tedious. Eclipse acts as a client to the control versioning software server. Even if you are already using a third-party client tool to interface with the versioning server, it can be a hassle to switch back and forth between the tool and the Eclipse development environment. The integrated Eclipse client eliminates this switching and is one of the most elegant CVS clients available.

In this chapter, we will go through setting up Eclipse to use CVS and Subversion. We do not assume any prior experience with versioning systems, so at first, the information will be very basic and introductory. Later, we will focus on setting up Eclipse and tour more advanced integration features.

We do not have to do any installations on the Eclipse side. Eclipse includes a CVS client in the JDT package. In addition to the Eclipse CVS client, we will also take a look at **Subclipse**, an Eclipse plug-in that is installed by PHPEclipse.

To work with the examples in this chapter, we will also need versioning system servers. We will briefly go through the installation, configuration, and processes for both CVS and Subversion. This will allow you to explore both the CVS plug-in and Subclipse, if you have one but not the other, or if you have neither. Both CVS and Subversion are rich and complex subjects. If you are going to actually set up a CVS or Subversion server for production use, there are plenty of books and resources that go through both products thoroughly.

Installing and Setting Up CVS

If you need a CVS server to use with Eclipse, follow these instructions. The goal of these instructions is to install and configure a CVS server as quickly as possible. The way this is accomplished varies by operating system. There is a difference in the actual CVS software package and slight variation in the connection method used. This is because we are going to leverage the software already installed on some systems and configuration shortcuts available on others. Regardless of which method you use, please note that we are taking some liberties with respect to best practices and security. These directions are only to be used in a development and learning environment, and not a production environment. If you are setting up a CVS server for actual production use, first and foremost, do not run it on a local workstation, and second, use a dedicated CVS book to help you with configuration and installation.

Windows Installation

CVS has been modified into a free and easy-to-use package called **CVSNT**. March Hare is a commercial venture that sells support for CVSNT. CVSNT includes some easy-to-use administrative GUI tools and additional commands to enhance CVS. It is also available for Mac OS X and Linux; however, GUI tools are only available on Windows.

1. Go to http://www.march-hare.com/cvsnt to download this package. After you download CVSNT, run the installer. The installer will guide you through the installation process. Accept the recommended installation suggestions and recommended location. Make a note of where the software was installed because we might need to access this in the next step. You will have to restart your machine after the installation.

2. Launch the CVSNT Control Panel. The installer should have created a shortcut to the CVSNT Control Panel in your Start menu and Desktop. Double-click on this. If these shortcuts were not installed, go to the folder where CVSNT was installed and double-click on the file named cvsnt.cpl. You will be greeted with the CVSNT welcome screen:

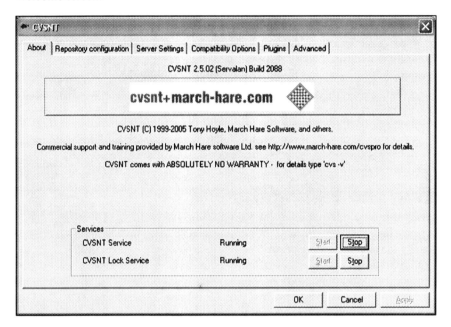

Immediately we can see that the CVSNT service is up and running. In future, to start or stop CVSNT, you can come back to this screen and use the Start and Stop buttons.

3. Create a repository. Click on the Repository configuration tab. This tab lists all the repositories on your machine. Unless you have special needs for security and permissions, you typically need just one repository. All your applications will reside as projects underneath that repository.

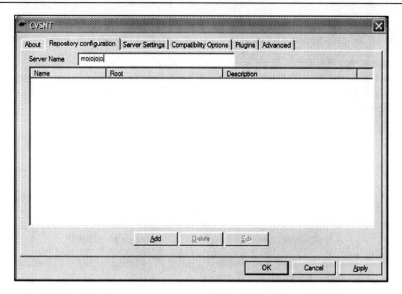

Click on the Add button to add a repository. This will take you to a dialog box to enter your repository settings.

4. Enter your repository settings. Most importantly, you will specify a location for the repository. In this example we place it on the c: drive, but you can place it just about anywhere that is not being used for anything else. When you type the location path, or use the Browse button to specify the location, CVSNT will automatically populate the name of the repository. Notice that the name is basically the path to the repository, but without the drive letter. This is because CVS was originally a UNIX program, where drive letters do not exist. In UNIX, to refer to a repository, we use the directory path. For compatibility with client programs and the CVS protocol, we use the name to refer to the repository in CVSNT.

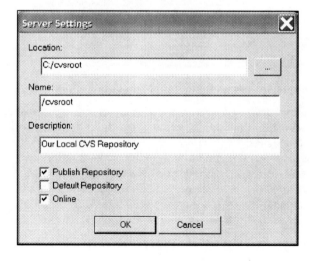

Enter a description for the directory. If this repository is the only repository on this workstation, click the Default Repository checkbox. Otherwise, you can accept the default settings.

5. Create the repository directory if necessary. After you click the OK button, CVSNT will try to create the CVSROOT directory and all necessary meta-files in the repository directory. If the repository directory does not exist, CVSNT will prompt you on whether it should create the directory. Click Yes to accept the option:

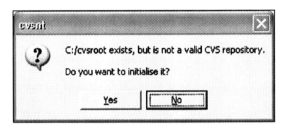

Once this is done, you can see that the repository has been added to the list of available repositories. Click OK to exit this screen:

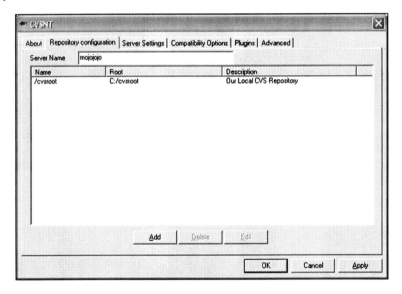

6. Add yourself as a **pserver** user. In CVS, we have several options to connect to the server. pserver was one of the first methods and still commonly used. SSH is very popular due to the need for security. For CVSNT, we will use pserver to connect to the server because we would have to do additional installations and configurations under Windows for SSH. If you do decide to eventually set up a CVS server, be aware of the security issues with pserver. While very flexible and compatible, it does not offer very tough security. One example is that it keeps its own user and password list. While this can give you better control, it's also not hard to decrypt. To add

yourself as a pserver user, drop into the command prompt in Windows. Use the `passwd` command to enter yourself. You must have a real Windows account on the machine, and you must use this name after the −r flag. This −r flag denotes an alias to a real system user name. This is very important, especially if your login name is just an alias to the administrator account. The −a flag tells CVS to add the user name. For simplicity, we keep this the same as what we entered for the −r flag.

```
C:\Documents and Settings\Shu> cvs passwd −r shu −a shu
Adding user shu
New Password:
Verify Password:

C:\Documents and Settings\Shu>
```

After you enter a user name, you will be prompted to enter and verify a password.

That's it for installing and configuring a CVS server under Windows. You can go ahead and skip to the discussion on *The CVS Repository Perspective*.

Macintosh Installation

The easiest way to install and configure CVS on a Macintosh is to install the **Apple XCode Developer Tools**. These tools include a CVS server. When XCode is installed, the CVS package is automatically configured and runs at startup. To get XCode, visit `http://developer.apple.com`. You will have to register as an Apple developer. The free, basic level of membership allows you to download XCode for free.

After you download XCode, just run the installation package to install the CVS Server. The installation also includes goodies not part of the standard OS X installation, including the XCode IDE for Mac OS X development, Ruby, and Python.

The drawback to this method is that the version of CVS shipped before Tiger (Mac OS X 10.4) is a bit dated. Some of the more advanced features of Eclipse's version synchronization tools do not work. However, this version is more than adequate to do basic check-in/check-out of files. If you want all the team synchronization features, you will need to compile your own version of CVS or use Mac OS X 10.4 or later.

Linux Installation

CVS was originally a UNIX software package. Thus, it runs natively and is common in the Linux world. Your distribution should include an option to install and configure CVS automatically. If your distribution classifies the types of software it has available, check under development tools for CVS. If it does not include CVS, consult the CVS site or a book on CVS to install from source.

Macintosh and Linux Configuration

Under Macintosh and Linux, we have the luxury of using the SSH protocol to connect to CVS. This gives us better security with less user configuration. The drawback is that we do not have a GUI to create and initialize the server for us. We will have to do this by hand.

Drop into the command line and enter the following commands. We are assuming that you have root privileges when you enter these commands.

1. Decide on a `cvsroot` directory location. First and foremost, we need to specify a location for our repository. Often, this will be a place that can be a mount point in its own partition or drive, but it can be any location as long as the directory is not used for anything else. If necessary, create this directory:

   ```
   Buttercup:/Users/shuchow root# mkdir /var/lib/cvsroot
   ```

2. Initialize the repository directory. Next, we need to initialize the `cvsroot`. This marks the directory as an official CVS repository and places the CVSROOT directory under it. Be aware that you definitely need to have root privileges for this command to work. It is not enough just to have *write* permissions on the directory.

   ```
   Buttercup:/Users/shuchow root# cvs -d /var/lib/cvsroot init
   ```

   The –d parameter tells CVS where the `cvsroot` repository is. Sometimes you'll see documentation telling you to set an environment variable called CVSROOT with the value of the path to `cvsroot`. This is to let you skip the –d flag when entering command-line commands. Since we did not set the environment variable, we will have to pass the directory path. The `init` command tells CVS to initialize this directory as a `cvsroot` directory.

   CVS will send you a confirmation message that the directory has been initialized.

   ```
   cvs init: Repository /var/lib/cvsroot initialized
   ```

3. Change the owner of the repository directories to yourself. We are now going to pass ownership of the `cvsroot` directory back to ourselves, and make sure all subdirectories have the same permissions. Note that this is a shortcut we're taking so that our login can access `cvsroot`. Replace 'shuchow' with your account name.

   ```
   Buttercup:/Users/shuchow root# chown -R shuchow cvsroot
   Buttercup:/Users/shuchow root# chmod u+s cvsroot
   ```

CVS is now set up and we're ready to store some source code.

The CVS Repository Perspective

Eclipse manages CVS functionality in the CVS Repository perspective. The perspective is made up of four views:

- CVS Repositories manages all the repositories you use.
- CVS Annotate gives you information about a file.
- CVS Resource History shows you when a version of a file was added, who added it, and the changes that were made.
- CVS Editors shows you who saved, or committed, the file to the repository and when it was done.

To get a better understanding of what these views do, we should have an example to work with in the repository. To do this, let's configure Eclipse to use the local repository we just initialized, and upload our ShelterSite project into CVS.

Adding a Repository

To add a repository, open the CVS Repositories view of the CVS Repository perspective. By default, it should appear where the Navigator is on the left side of the Workbench.

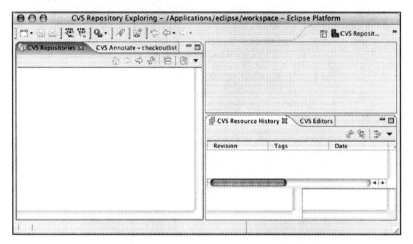

Right-click in the CVS Repositories pane and select New | Repository Location… You can also click the Add CVS Repository icon (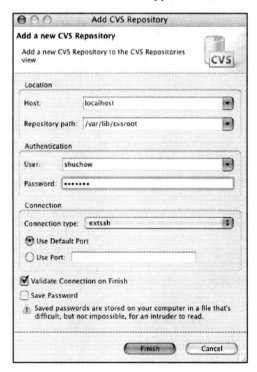) in the toolbar. You will be presented with the Add CVS Repository wizard. This screenshot is that of an SSH-type connection:

The first section asks about location. We're going to put localhost in the Host field and the path we declared to be cvsroot in the Repository path field. If you are using a remote CVS server, ask the server administrator what these settings are.

If you look further down to Connection, you'll see that we're using extssh as the Connection Type. This is an SSH-style connection. This means that we will basically log into the machine using our regular account. We will need to enter our account details in the User and Password fields. If you are using the pserver connection method, you may have a separate login account for CVS.

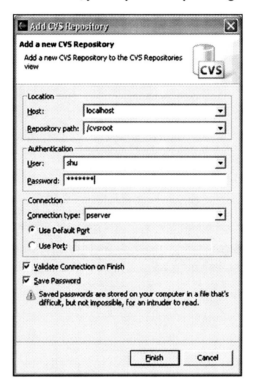

If you have been following along with our example under Windows, your dialog box should look like the one above. Note that we use the name of the repository, not the path to the repository itself (c:/cvsroot), in the Repository path field. Remember this is because CVSNT creates an alias from the UNIX-style directory path (which does not have a drive letter) to the Windows-style directory path for compatibility.

Click on the Finish button to add this repository. Your repository should now be added under the CVS Repositories view. If you expand the directory tree, you will see all of the available projects underneath the repository. The directory tree is separated into the Head trunk and Branches.

Expand the Head trunk to see the available projects in Head. So far, there should be only one—CVSROOT, and that is because by default, it is a directory underneath c:/cvsroot. Expand CVSROOT and you'll see the files available underneath the project:

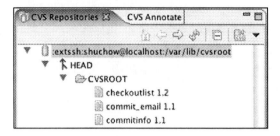

Adding a Project to CVS

CVSROOT is interesting, but we really shouldn't play with these files. We should add our own project, ShelterSite, into CVS and use it as part of our development process.

> Remember, CVSROOT (all uppercase) is the project's CVS metadata directory. cvsroot (all lowercase) is the root directory for CVS, where all the source files are stored.

To do this, we must first create a directory under cvsroot for our project. This will register our application as a project when Eclipse connects to it. You can name this directory anything you wish, but for simplicity's sake, it should at least be related to the project name in Eclipse, if not exactly the same.

Next, go back into the PHP perspective or Resource perspective. In the Navigator view, right-click on the name of the project, ShelterSite, and select Team | Share Project...; you will be taken to the first part of the Share Project wizard. The Team menu item is where Eclipse keeps all of the CVS commands. This option will be used frequently in this chapter.

Select CVS from the options available and click on the **Next** button. If you have any other versioning system plug-ins installed, such as the Subversion plug-in that comes with PHPEclipse, they will be available here.

Next, select the repository that you wish to use. This list is populated from your list of repositories in the CVS Repositories view. You can select one of the repositories available here, or you can select **Create a new repository location** to drop into the **Add Repository** wizard.

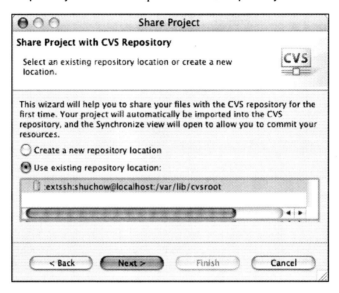

Select the repository that we have set up. Click on the **Next** button to continue.

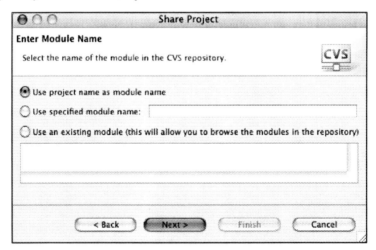

In this step, we select the name with which we want to store the application in CVS. If you named the CVS project directory the same as the Eclipse project name, you can select the first option. If you gave the directory a different name, you can select **Use specified module name** and specify this existing directory. To browse through the available projects in CVS, select Use an existing module. You will be presented with a list of available directories under cvsroot.

Eclipse will then ask you whether you want to check this into the Head trunk or a branch. Since this is the only copy of the source code right now, it will act as the master copy. Merge it into the Head.

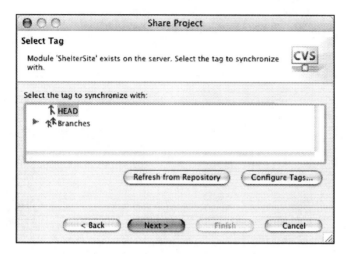

Click Next to do a final preview of your source code.

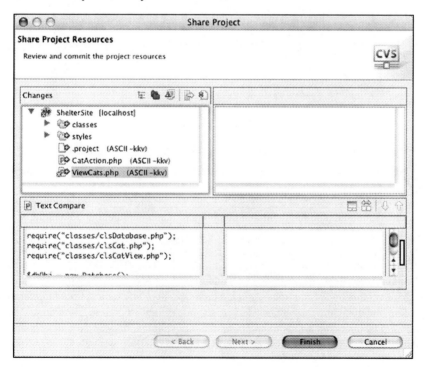

On the final confirmation screen you can review the files you are about to commit. Clicking the Finish button will confirm the creation of the project in CVS.

You will then be presented with one final screen to add comments and verify your commit. Eclipse does not require a comment on commits, but entering in something descriptive is definitely a good practice. We should always write a few sentences describing the changes that were made. Here, we are simply noting that this is the initial revision.

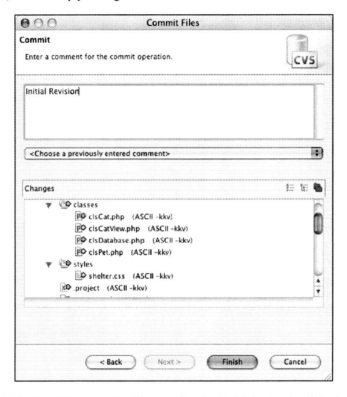

Click on the Finish button. The commit will start after the Finish button is clicked.

In the Navigator view, your project name will indicate that it is tied to a CVS server by the server name appearing as a label next to the project name.

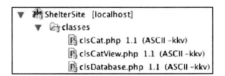

If you wish to sever this bond between your local copy and the CVS server, for example, in case of a repository server change, you can right-click on a project and select Team | Disconnect...The label of Disconnect is sort of misleading. If a project is tied to a repository, Eclipse does not actually persist a connection with the server. Eclipse merely remembers an association with the CVS server.

The number next to each source file is the version number, and the label mentions if the file is an ASCII text file or binary. The version number is the identity number that CVS uses to keep track of a file at a particular point. Version numbers automatically increment whenever you commit. The version number remains the same if you only save changes to a file.

Committing and Updating

Let's change one of our files in the project. Switch back to the PHP perspective. Open the viewCats.php page in the editor, we'll add a link to the webmaster at the bottom of the page.

```
</table>
Any questions? <a href="webmaster@sheltersite.org">email the webmaster!</a>
</body>
</html>
```

After saving this file, you will see an end bracket (>) before the name of the file in the Navigator view. This is often called the 'dirty flag'. This tells us that the file has been changed since the last update, and will need a commit. Modified files are referred to as 'dirty' while those in CVS are called 'clean'.

CatAction.php 1.1 (ASCII ~kkv)
> ViewCats.php 1.1 (ASCII ~kkv)

Committing will designate this file as the official and most recent version of the file. Anyone else that pulls this file from the repository will get this version. To commit the file, we will right-click on the file in the Navigator view and select Team | Commit...

You will then be prompted to enter in a comment about the file. After you enter a comment and click on the Finish button, the file will commit itself back into the repository.

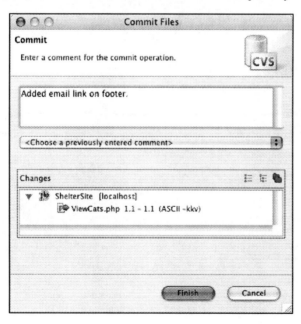

The dirty flag indicator in the Navigator view will disappear. You will also notice that there is a new, higher version number next to the file name. Every time a commit occurs, the version number is incremented.

In a situation where there is a central repository shared by many team members, if you commit a file, only you will have the latest version of the file. Other team members have an older version. In order for them to replace their local copy with the newer copy in the repository, they will have to update their local copies by going to Team | Update. Eclipse will compare the copy of the file in the repository with the copy of the file in the workspace. If the workspace copy and latest version match, it will skip the file. If workspace copy matches a previous version, then it will replace the workspace version with the latest copy from CVS. At the start of everyone's work session, everyone should use this Update feature to see what has changed in the application.

> Note that you can do both updates and commits on the project level. This will make Eclipse update or commit on every file in that project, including those in subdirectories.

If the workspace copy matches neither previous versions nor the current version, then there is a conflict. Eclipse will not overwrite the workspace copy, and instead, issue an alert asking you whether you wish to use the local copy, overwrite the local copy, or merge the two versions. The first two options should be self-explanatory. Merging will allow you to review the conflicts and manually resolve the issues. When you choose to merge, Eclipse will open the file in the editor and insert special characters to highlight conflicts throughout the source code. Here is an example of a typical conflict displayed by Eclipse:

```
10  $listingArr = $listingObj->getAllCatsArray($dbObj->getD
11
12  <<<<<<< ViewCats.php
13  // This comment is supposed to trigger a conflict
14
15  =======
16  // So is this conflict.
17
18  >>>>>>> 1.3
19  ?>
```

Workspace and CVS versions of changes are delimited with brackets (<, >) and equals signs (=). In the first set, we see the version on the workspace.

```
<<<<<<< ViewCats.php
// This comment is supposed to trigger a conflict

=======
```

In the second set, we see the version that was in CVS.

```
=======
// So is this conflict.

>>>>>>> 1.3
```

It is up to you to resolve the conflict. Will your code changes be accepted into the Head? Or will the changes made by a co-worker be accepted? CVS won't replace actual communication with people. However, before you can do that, you'll need to find out who posted the previous version. In order to find out this information, and information about the previous files in CVS, we'll need to visit the CVS Annotate and CVS Resource History views.

CVS Annotate View

CVS Annotate and CVS Resource History views work closely together to show the progression of a file. Let's make a small change in our source code to see how these two views can help us.

In our `clsCatView.php` class, we are going to add a small function to return an array with the fields of a cat when we pass it an ID number.

```php
public function getACat($id, $dbConn)
{
    $sql = "SELECT * FROM tCat WHERE CatID = " . $id;
    $e = mysql_query($sql, $dbConn);
    return mysql_fetch_array($e);
}
```

Save and commit this file. Your Navigator view should show that the local version is version number 1.2.

Right-click on the file and select Team | Show Annotation. This will activate the CVS Annotate view.

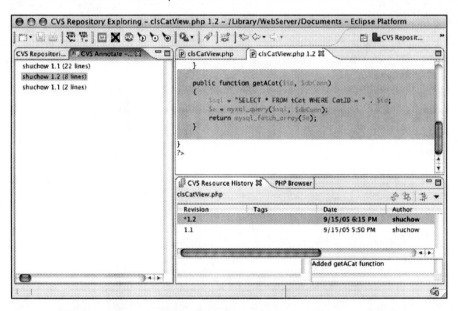

By default, the CVS Annotate view appears on the left side of the Workbench. It's a rather simple view. The philosophy of this view is to show you the file as it currently stands and how it got there. This view sections out the file and gives you a rough idea of what section was added in a revision and by whom. Click on a section in the CVS Annotate view and the code block in question will be highlighted in the editor.

CVS Resource History

CVS Resource History gives you more information on changes to a file with a different point of view. While CVS Annotate centers on the current state of the file, CVS Resource History shows the past incarnations of a file. In this view, you can see every version of the file, and compare them against each other. You will see this view below the editor:

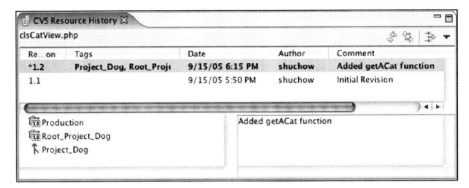

A row of the view shows you the version of the file, tags (which we will take a look at shortly), the date and time of commit, who committed the file, and the comments they entered. We see each tag and branch that the file belongs to in the **Tag Viewer** on the left, and the complete comments in the **Comment Viewer** on the right. Both viewers can be turned on and off in this pane's option menu.

This view has a very helpful line-by-line comparison feature for your source code. With it, you can compare the exact differences between two versions. To use it, highlight the two versions you want to compare (use the *Shift* key to select the second file), right-click on one of them, and select Compare. Eclipse will launch a text viewer with both versions shown side by side.

The viewer highlights any missing text on one side, and points to the location where it would be on the other file. In this example, our new function would be right underneath the closing curly bracket in the old file. If you deleted lines in a newer file, this comparison would be the same, but in the opposite direction. The deleted block would be highlighted and the pointer line would show you where the code block was in the earlier version.

This feature requires at least CVS 1.11 or greater to work. For Macintosh users, this means you will need to be on Mac OS 10.4, Tiger, to get this version with XCode. On older versions of Mac OS X, you will have to compile your own version of CVS from source.

Tagging

Along the way of your development process, you will release your code to testing, to production, and maybe ship it off to another team. It would be good to have a note that could be sent along with the code. CVS allows you to place a version tag on files. Tagging is more than just notes, though. It tells everyone that a certain group of files are related to each other. For example, if you work on a web application that contains one hundred files, and you're working on a new feature that touches half of those files, come deployment time, it would be nice to know which of those fifty files need to be pushed out. You could just write them on a piece of paper, but tagging is a more eloquent way of doing this.

Let's say our current project is in production. We would like to make a note of that fact, so that if there are any problems later on, we can remove all files of later versions that do not have this tag. There are other advantages to tagging. You may have noticed that at certain points, Eclipse asks you where you want to do certain things, like comparisons and retrievals. It gives you the options to do it on the Head, a branch, or a version. So far, we've been doing this on the Head. However, we could do these things on a version. If you are working on a branch, and you want to do a file comparison on a file that was in the Head last year, you can do this with ease. Meanwhile, you are not touching the code in Head at all.

To place a tag, in the Navigator right-click on the project and select Team | Tag As Version. You will be presented with the Tag Resources dialog box:

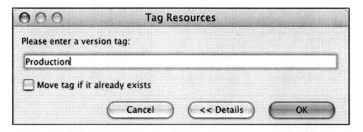

Give this tag a name. There are certain restrictions with tag names. They must start with a letter and can only contain letters, numbers, underscores, or hyphens. Other than that you can, and should, create your own naming convention for tags. If the tag name already exists, click on the Move tag if it already exists checkbox to move the tag to the new version that you are trying to tag now. Click the OK button to create the tag. CVS does this very discretely. You will be returned to the perspective you were just working in, and you will not see any visible changes in CVS.

Branching

Branching is similar to version tagging, except for a significant difference—it separates the code from the Head. Therefore, you can continue to work on it without affecting the code that is used in production. When we are done, we will use Eclipse to merge this code back into the Head. Let's walk through a sample scenario.

Let's assume that we are adding a feature to view adoptable dogs. We will need to branch the code so that we don't interfere with the existing site. Right-click on the project name, ShelterSite, in the Navigator view. Select Team | Branch... This will bring up the Create a new CVS Branch dialog box:

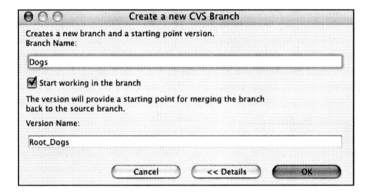

Here, we name the branch Dogs. CVS will also automatically create a Version Name. Click on the OK button and the branch will be created. Now, there are essentially two versions of the application in CVS. We will work on the branch to add a new feature. If someone needs to work on the Head, they can check it out without interfering with our work.

We will need a new Dog class. It will be very similar to the Cat class, except whatever says Cat needs to be replaced with Dog. Drop back into the PHP perspective to create this file. You can just do a Save As on the clsCat.php file, name it clsDog.php, and place it in the same directory. The only difference from clsCat.php will be the first few lines of the file. The changes are highlighted in the code shown below:

```php
<?php
  require_once("clsPet.php");
  class Dog extends Pet
  {
    private $dogID;
    private $name;
    private $gender;
    private $age;
    private $breed;
    public function setDogID($dogID) { $this->dogID = $dogID; }
    public function getDogID() { return $this->dogID; }
```

Now save and commit this file. Eclipse will see that the clsDog.php file is not in the CVS repository and ask you if you want to add it. Click Yes. Enter a comment when Eclipse requests one. You may want to make a note that the new Dog class was added with this commit.

You can't see it right now, but CVS is now maintaining two copies of the source code. The first is the Head portion. The second is the Dog branch. How can you be certain of this without taking it on faith? A quick way to verify that there are two versions is to check out the branch and Head from CVS into new projects. This way, you can also see how Eclipse can pull entire projects from CVS. The steps below show how to create a branch of your code:

1. In the Navigator view, create a new project. Give it a distinctive name such as ShelterSite-Head.

2. Go to File | Import... to start the import wizard. Here, you can see the various storage mediums that Eclipse can talk to. For this example, we want to Checkout Projects from CVS, so click on it. Click on the Next button.

3. Select the repository that we created. Click on the Next button.

4. In the Select Module dialog box select the ShelterSite module. You can do this by typing the exact name in the Use specified module name box, or you can browse through the modules in the repository through the Use an existing module option. At this point, the Finish button will be enabled, but don't click on it. Instead, click on the Next button.

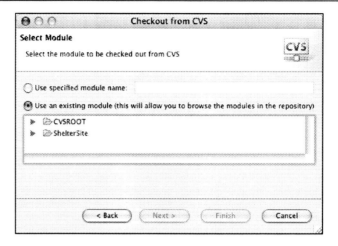

5. In the Check Out As box select Check out into an existing project and click Next. Select the project that we want to check out the files into, the ShelterSite-Head project. Let the Target folder name remain as ShelterSite. Click on the Next button.

6. Finally, we will be on the last screen of the wizard, where we can select the tag to choose:

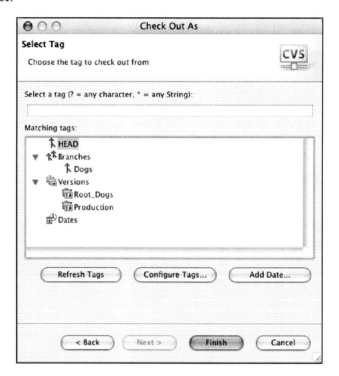

Generally, a dialog like this will always appear while working on options like checkouts, specialized commits, and import/exports. This dialog box allows us to specify for what version of a project to put or pull code. We want to check out the code base for the Head, so highlight that and click on the Finish button.

In your Navigator view, you will now see that the ShelterSite-Head project is filled with a copy of the application without the clsDog.php file. You can also repeat this exercise with the Dog branch to see a complete version of the application with the clsDog class.

Merging

Merging is the practice of merging two sets of code bases. While Eclipse can help us do this, it is still a very manual process, requiring at least one developer to work on it. Often this is a two-person process, with one developer being the expert on one code base, and the other being the expert on the other.

In this example, we will compare the Dog branch with the Head branch for eventual merging of our changes back into the Head. However, as we've seen, by leveraging tags and other branches, we are really not restricted in what we compare. Often, developers merge their branches together before merging into the Head.

In some environments, regular developers are not allowed to touch the Head. That job goes to a source keeper, who reviews each and every change that goes into the Head. Developers can only work on branches.

Initiate merging by selecting a project in the Navigator view and right-clicking on it. Select Team | Merge... You will be asked what two versions you are comparing.

After you have selected the two projects, you are taken to the Team Synchronization perspective.

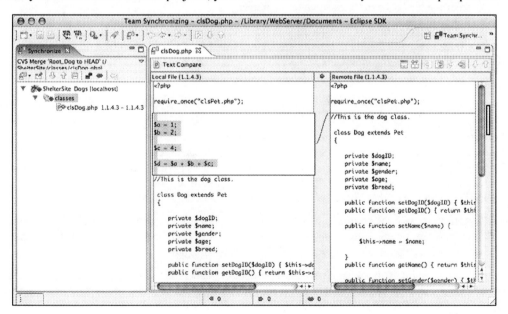

Here, we can go through each of our changes. Eclipse automatically does a comparison of the two projects. Each difference is listed in Synchronize view. Using this view, we can rotate through the reported differences. For any change that is accepted, we can simply click on the Update All Incoming Changes icon ( ).

Subclipse

Subversion is a versioning system that was created to modernize versioning needs and address some of the shortcomings of CVS. There are several key differences with Subversion and CVS. Some of the advantages Subversion has over CVS include:

- **Better speed**: Subversion is a newer code base designed with the newer techniques.
- **Better features and flexibility**: The repository is a database. This gives us more features and flexibility such as transactions.
- **Better handling of binary files**: CVS was originally built for storing text files.
- **Better handling of directories**: In CVS, keeping track of directories is not easy. Subversion addressed directory versions.
- **Better security**: Subversion has better safeguards against corruption on large projects. CVS can be prone to problems on projects over 100 files in size.
- **Better integration**: Subversion offers out-of-the-box integration with **WebDAV** to serve your repository over a web browser.
- **Reduced learning curve**: Subversion works very similarly to CVS, thereby reducing the learning curve.

On the other hand, CVS still holds many advantages:

- **CVS is ubiquitous**: CVS has been around for a long time. If a third-party program interfaces with a versioning system, chances are that CVS is one of the top, and often the only, systems it integrates.
- **Less flexibility with the stored code**: While storing the code in a database gives us new features, it truly makes things a lot more complicated. No longer can we go into an archive file and edit meta-files manually to fix problems.

Subclipse is the open source plug-in designed to interface with Subversion servers. While the standard download of Eclipse includes the CVS integration package, Subclipse is installed by the PHPEclipse plug-in. Luckily for us, the behavioral similarities between Subversion and CVS carry over to Subclipse and the CVS plug-in. When you use Subclipse, you will notice that the knowledge you have of the CVS Repository perspective will come in handy.

In this section, we will take a quick look at the SVN perspective. You will notice that it is very similar in look and functionality to the CVS perspective. Very often, the only difference between the two views is the label 'SVN' instead of 'CVS' on view title tabs.

The examples we will use hook into the main repository of the Subclipse project. If you wish, you can download and install Subversion yourself. The project site is at http://subversion.tigris.org. The

Subversion team has done an excellent job creating pre-compiled binaries for a wide variety of platforms. In addition, the product is very well documented. Two very good resources are the site itself and a free PDF version of a Subversion book available at `http://svnbook.red-bean.com/`.

Viewing a Subversion Project

We will need to add the Subclipse project site to our list of available repositories. In the CVS perspective, we did this with the CVS Repository view. In Subclipse, we will do the same thing, but from the SVN Repository view. One key difference is the Add SVN Repository dialog box. SVN handles connections differently to CVS. The difference is subtle, but philosophically important. Instead of a connection method (pserver, SSH, extssh), SVN requires you to specify the type of repository at the other end. The connection method is automatically determined by the client.

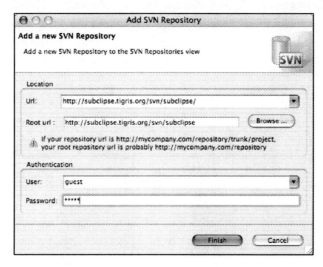

To log into the Subclipse project site, enter `http://subclipse.tigris.org/svn/subclipse` as the Url. You will have to hit the Browse button and select the Root URL. You cannot directly type this information into the text box. The username and password for a view-only account is guest/guest.

Eclipse will connect to the repository, and you will receive the list of files for the project in your SVN Repository view.

If the Subversion repository is using a WebDAV server, you can import the file using the WebDAV protocol. Be aware that on the list of available import source types, the option will not be explicitly stated as Subclipse, but instead is marked as a WebDAV server.

As you go through this project, you will see the similarities with the CVS Perspective. You can commit and update the same way, and there are two views—SVN Resource History and SVN Annotations—that operate the same way as the CVS Resource History and CVS Annotations. However, Subclipse is not an exact clone of the CVS plug-in. Subclipse is specialized for SVN when there are differences. You will see that version numbers do not have decimal points, and that directories now have version numbers.

Summary

Source code control is one of the most important steps of development. It is often forgotten because it is one of the last steps and requires a bit of discipline in usage. However, like a nightly backup, you will appreciate it the most when you need it. Eclipse interfaces with two very popular versioning systems, CVS and Subversion. Eclipse acts as a client to these systems, making tasks easier and making us more likely to use version control.

In this chapter, we saw how Eclipse interfaces with CVS repositories and SVN repositories through plug-ins. We installed CVS on our local machine. CVS interfacing is given to us by the CVS Repository plug-in, which is included with the Eclipse SDK. We walked through setting up a CVS repository. In doing so, we gained a greater understanding of how versioning repositories work. We added our project to CVS and practiced updating, committing, branching, and merging.

SVN is an open source versioning system designed to address some of the shortcomings of CVS. However, it shares a lot of the same end-user behavior as CVS to make the transition simpler. We used the Subclipse plug-in, which is included with PHPEclipse, to interact with SVN. Although different systems, the Subclipse plug-in works in similar ways and shares a similar set of philosophies with the CVS plug-in.

8
Deploying Your Site

We've walked through the complete process of web development using Eclipse, from development to code storage. The final part would be to deploy your site to a web server. Once again, Eclipse simplifies our work by including several tools that aid us in this process.

The key to deployment in Eclipse is the **export** function. Eclipse gives us many options in exporting our site. First, we will look at **FTP**, an old and common method of moving files. **WebDAV** is an interesting way to upload files using a web server. **Secure FTP (SFTP)**, a protocol similar to FTP, but encrypted, is enjoying immense popularity in this security-conscious age. FTP and WebDAV exports are provided through plug-ins as part of the PHPEclipse package. The **Klomp** plug-in gives us SFTP export capabilities, and comes bundled with PHPEclipse.

Finally, we will see how **Ant**, traditionally regarded as a Java tool, can help us in PHP deployment.

Setting Up a Test FTP Server

A server running FTP, SFTP, or WebDAV processes is a fairly common thing. However, if you do not have a server available for experimentation with Eclipse, you can easily set up these services. However, as of Eclipse 3.0/3.1, these clients do not work when connecting to a local server. You will have to set up a second machine on your local network to run these services. To help you, we will touch on how to quickly set up an FTP server.

Again, a word of caution—these instructions are designed to give us a crude but effective file server. It will neither be very secure nor optimized for performance. If you need a production FTP server, consult other resources on configuring your machine and security best practices.

To start off, decide on an upload area. This directory could be anywhere, but be sure you have *read* and *write* permissions to that directory.

Windows

On the Windows platform, you can place a copy of the XAMPP package on your server. XAMPP includes FileZilla, an easy-to-manage, open source FTP client and server package. First, make sure the FTP server is running by checking the XAMPP Control Panel. The status for FileZilla should be set to Running. Inside the main xampp directory there will be a FileZillaFTP directory.

In here, you'll find an executable named **FileZilla Server Interface**. This program provides a GUI front-end to any FileZilla FTP server, local, or remote. Launch this application. You'll be presented with a dialog box to choose your FTP server:

This application automatically lets you administer your local instance of FileZilla. Click on the OK button to accept the default options.

You'll be taken to the main administration screen, which is essentially a console for the FTP server. We need to add ourselves as an FTP user to this system, so click on Edit | Users to pull up the main Users administration screen.

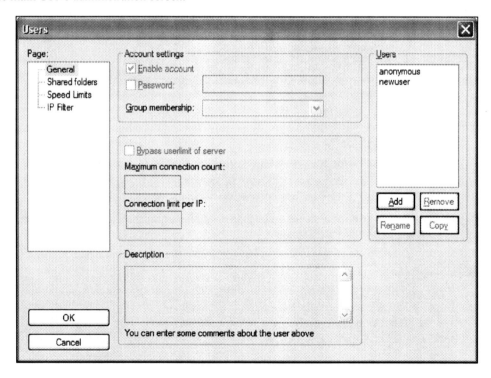

Under the Users listing, click on the Add button. Specify a login name. When we approve the addition, we'll be taken back to the Users administration screen. At this time, it would be prudent to add a password to our account in the Account Settings section. Next, we need to specify the home directory of our account. Make sure the newly added account is selected on the Users listing, and then select the Shared folders listing on the right, under Page.

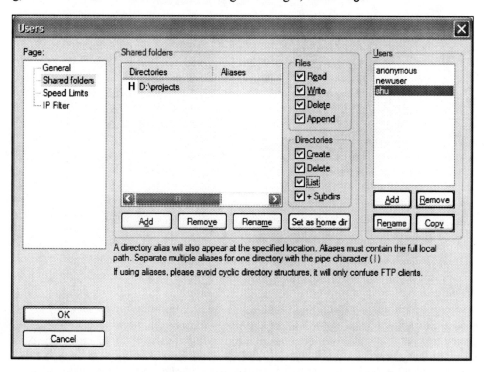

In the Shared folders area, click on the Add button. Browse to a directory that you selected as your publishing directory. This should be the same directory as your Apache document root. If this is the first directory that you added through the FileZilla Server Interface, it will automatically receive an **H** icon next to the name in the Shared folders box. This designates that the directory is the home directory for the user, and at every logon, the user will automatically be re-routed to that directory after login. Before you click the OK button, make sure all the permissions checkboxes are checked for the publishing directory. FTP services run on TCP port 21, and FileZilla will open that port for use. If you are using Windows XP, a system dialog box might appear, asking whether you are sure you wish to unblock the port. Click the OK button to allow the unblocking.

Macintosh

Mac OS X includes an FTP/SFTP server built in. The server is also preconfigured for our needs, using the users and groups of the local machine. We won't have to do any extra setup. However, it is turned off by default. To turn on the server, go to System Preferences | Sharing. Make sure the checkbox next to FTP Access is checked.

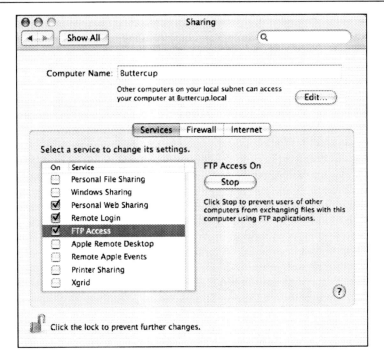

Linux

An FTP daemon is a basic component of a Linux server, and your distribution should have one installed or available to install. Unfortunately, it may not always be started and configured on your Linux distribution. Also, how you start and configure differs greatly by distribution. The GUI clients will differ if you are using Gnome or KDE desktops. Some distributions include a GUI client to administer FTP services, while others need to be administered by manually editing configuration text files and stopped and started via the command line. Consult your distribution's documentation for instructions.

FTP, SFTP, and WebDAV Export

FTP, SFTP, and WebDAV exports are very similar. They follow the same flow and use almost the same screens. To trigger an export, select the project in the Navigator view and click on the File | Export... menu option. This will give you a list of export options to select from.

The Klomp plug-in gives us the ability to export via SFTP. Unfortunately, as of this writing, it does not work with the latest version of Eclipse, version 3.1. If you absolutely need a secure way to transfer files and Klomp does not work with your version of Eclipse, you might consider using WebDAV over the `https://` protocol, or Ant using SFTP.

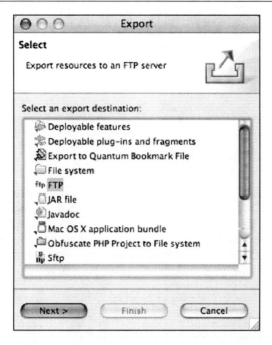

Most of the options in this list are installed by the JDT and are Java related. Some allow you to export settings to be shared between team members. A handful, like FTP, Sftp, and WebDAV, are actually related to moving source files to another area. Select FTP and click on the Next button to continue.

If you get an error message saying 'unable to load class' you will have to download drops containing FTP and WebDAV target management support plug-ins from the Eclipse site. Go to the Eclipse download site `http://download.eclipse.org/eclipse/downloads/` and click on your version; you will find the drops for FTP and WebDAV Support on that page. Download and copy all the contents of the `features` and `plugins` directories into the `features` and `plugins` directories of your Eclipse installation.

The next screen will ask if you wish to export a project that you previously exported via FTP:

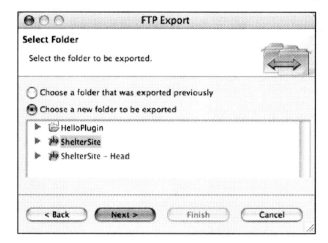

When you are first presented with this screen and if you have not done this before, the text area will be empty. Click on the Choose a new project to be exported radio button and you will be presented with a list of all the projects in your workspace. Select the ShelterSite project and click the Next button to continue. Eclipse will create a deployment mapping for this project. When you export again in the future, Eclipse reads this mapping to the server settings associated with a project, saving you a few of the following steps to choose a server.

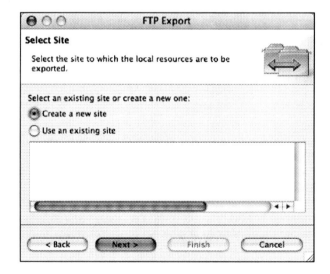

Similar to the last screen, this screen will ask if you want to export the project to a location to which you previously exported, or if you want to export to a new location. Again, if you have never exported via FTP before, the list area will be blank. Choose Create a new site and click on Next, this will launch the Create a connection to an FTP site dialog box.

All of your FTP, SFTP, and WebDAV locations on this screen can be edited and deleted from the Site Explorer view. Access this view by going to the Window | Show View... | Other... | Target Management | Site Explorer menu option.

Enter your server connection settings here. Click the Next button to continue. If you are using WebDAV or SFTP, this screen will be different. However, all three will essentially ask you for the same details, like server name and authentication.

On the final screen in the export wizard, you will have a chance to decide which files you want to upload. You can select individual files, or upload the entire project into the remote directory by checking the correlating checkbox next to the item. If the site has been previously uploaded, you can also do a line-by-line code comparison of the project.

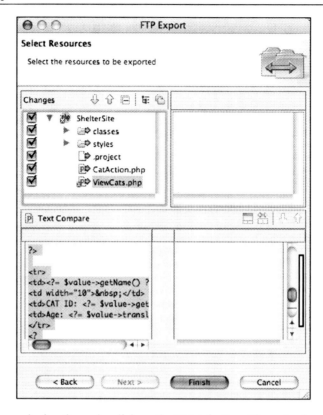

After you are done analyzing the code, click on the Finish button. The upload process will begin at this point. After this step, your site will be uploaded to the remote server, and you will be taken back to the development perspective.

Using Ant for Deployment

You may have heard of **Ant** in the Java development world. Being a pure Java tool, Ant is often called 'the Java version of make'. With Ant, you create scripts called **build files** that are interpreted by the **Ant parser**. These scripts aid you in Java development by compiling your code and deploying it in your build directory. For both small home-grown projects and large Java enterprise environments, Ant has become an absolutely critical tool for Java developers. In the PHP world, though, we do not have any code to compile, and often, FTP is adequate for moving files into production. Why, then, as PHP developers, do we care about Ant?

In some business environments, production web servers are tightly controlled. Developers are not allowed anywhere near the servers, let alone pushing out code at their whim. The sheer act of deploying new code often occurs only after a long ritual of meetings and approvals at various levels. In these environments, deployment occurs with a script that automates the delivery of an application from one area to the production site. Ant scripts can do this job for you for applications in any language.

Even if you are not working in such an environment, why would you use Ant? A key benefit is Ant's integration with CVS and Subversion. Using Ant, you can write a script to grab all files in the repository with a certain tag and FTP them to a production server. Imagine the time saved and reduction in human error with this. In a large application with PHP class files in one directory, HTML view files in another, JavaScript files in their own separate directory, and stylesheets in yet another, a deployment involves a huge effort and it is difficult to keep track of what has changed.

At deployment time, you have to check out all the correct files from CVS or Subversion and then FTP all of them again to the production web server. If all you have to do is tag a file at the end of testing, you have drastically reduced the chance that you'll miss something when retrieving from the code repository or FTPing.

Finally, Ant scripts are easy to write. Being XML-based, these scripts are fairly simple and intuitive. If we were not concerned with code cleanliness, it would take only one line of code to check out a project from the code repository, and another line to FTP files. The reference documentation is excellent. If you require any more support, Ant is supported by a large user base and online community. Being an Apache Foundation project doesn't hurt its popularity either.

Eclipse integrates Ant smoothly into our development environment. Included with the JDT, Eclipse has a nice Ant editor, templates, and tag help. You can execute them directly from Eclipse. Let's walk through an example using CVS.

> The official Ant release does not support Subversion. Luckily, Ant employs an extensible architecture like Eclipse. Tigris.org, the developer of Subversion, has created an Ant task called **SvnAnt** that allows Ant to interface with Subversion repositories. More information about this project is available at
> `http://subclipse.tigris.org/svnant.html`.

Setting up Ant for FTP

Before we get started, we need to install some additional files for Ant. FTP ability is an optional **Ant task** that is not included with the default installation of Eclipse. We need to download these files and add them to our Ant classpaths in Eclipse.

The steps required are:

1. Download and unzip the latest binaries of `commons-net.jar` and `commons-oro.jar`.
2. Install the `commons-net` and `commons-oro`.
3. Add these new files to the Ant classpath.

Downloading

You can find the `commons-net.jar` and `commons-oro.jar` files at `http://jakarta.apache.org/site/downloads/downloads_commons-net.cgi` and `http://jakarta.apache.org/site/downloads/downloads_oro.cgi` respectively.

You will need at least version 1.4.0 for `commons-net.jar` and at least version 2.0.8 for `commons-oro.jar`. When you expand the downloaded files, the JARs should have the version numbers as part of the file names, like `commons-net-1.4.0.jar`. This is perfectly acceptable and there is no need to change the file names.

Installing

Place these files in a clear location. It is recommended to create a new directory under the Eclipse installation folder called `antjars`. If you explore the Eclipse installation directory, you will find that the Ant plug-in is stored in its own folder under the `plugins` directory. This folder contains the original `commons-net.jar` and `commons-oro.jar`. These are the JARs that do not have our necessary FTP classes. You could replace these files, but it is generally not a good idea to fiddle with the default files. Therefore, we're going to place our replacement JARs outside the area having the default Eclipse-installed files. This way, Eclipse can still manage its own installed files, and if we upgrade, we don't lose any functionality because the user settings remember our classpath changes.

Adding Files to the Ant Classpath

By naming these files in the Ant classpath, we are telling Eclipse of their existence, and that critical JARs may be found in them. To add them to the classpath, go to the Window | Preferences | Ant | Runtime menu option. Click on Ant Home Entries (Default) in the list under Classpath. Click on the Add External Jars… button.

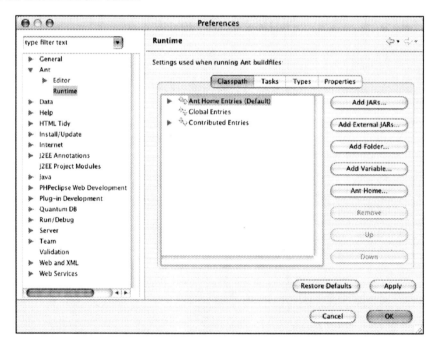

Select the two new JARs that you just downloaded. Click on the OK button. Our installation of Ant is now FTP enabled.

Creating Our Sample Ant Build File

In this demonstration, we will make a script to actually do what we have described. Our script will log into CVS, pull files from the Head of our project, put the files locally in a temporary directory, FTP the files into a web server, and finally do some cleaning up by deleting our temporary directory.

Generally, Ant scripts are composed of targets. Targets are basically groupings of commands called tasks. In order to be functional, each target contains at least one Ant task. These tasks are listed and explained in the official Ant documentation. A target might contain the task of compiling a Java program. At the beginning of the Ant file, we ordain one target as the special default target. Normally, when you run an Ant file, you pass it the target that you want to execute. If it doesn't have one, it will execute the default target.

We are going to create an Ant file with four targets. The first will check out the project from CVS into our local machine. The next will upload the files to a web server. The third target will delete the copy of the application that we downloaded from CVS. Our default target sits above these three. Its job will be to call the previous three targets in the correct order.

First, create a file in our project called `build.xml`. This is the standard name for Ant build files. This script has already been included in the sample code, so you do not have to type everything in manually. However, we will walk through the build file in its entirety and look at it section by section. You may want to pull up the complete file to follow along.

```xml
<?xml version="1.0" encoding="UTF-8"?>
  <project name="Deployment Script"
           default="startPublish"
           basedir=".">
```

This is the beginning of the Ant file. We include in a proper XML declaration here for good form. Ant files begin and end with a `<project>` tag. The important part of this tag is the `default` attribute. The `default` attribute tells the Ant engine which target to run if one is not specified when the build file is executed from the command line. You must declare this target later on in the file. While not officially required, Eclipse needs it to run build files because it automatically fires build files as-is. In other words, Eclipse does not prompt you for a target. Further, it is good coding practice to include a default.

```xml
<target name="startPublish">
  <antcall target="getFilesFromCVS" />
  <antcall target="StartFTP" />
  <antcall target="cleanUp" />
</target>
```

The code snippet shown above is our first target, named `startPublish`. We separate our deployment process into three separate tasks—check the files out from CVS into our temporary area, FTP them to our server, and finally clean up our temporary area. The `startPublish` target merely calls the other tasks in the correct order. Calling other targets is done by the `antcall` tag, which includes a mandatory target to call defined by the `target` attribute.

```xml
<target name="getFilesFromCVS">
  <cvs cvsRoot=":local:/var/lib/cvsroot"
       package="ShelterSite"
       dest="/tmp" />
</target>
```

This is our second target, getFilesFromCVS. There is only one task, cvs. This task pulls files from a CVS repository. The cvsRoot attribute defines the repository based on the CVS connection string. We specify a package to check out in the package attribute, and the dest attribute specifies the local directory where we want to place the checked out files.

> We briefly talked about CVS connection strings in the previous chapter. Here, we use the local connection method to connect to our local CVS server. This method is simple and easy, but only works on a CVS repository that is on our machine. Consult your CVS administrator or CVS documentation on how to construct a proper connection string for your server setup.

```
<target name="startFTP">
    <ftp server="127.0.0.1"
         userid="shuchow"
         password="TopSecretPassword!"
         remotedir="/Library/WebServer/Documents/test/"
         action="send">
```

The interaction with the FTP server is contained in the third target. First, we enter our connection settings in the appropriate attributes within the ftp tag. The attributes server and userid are your account credentials on the FTP server. While the FTP and SFTP export plug-ins in Eclipse do not work with local machines, Ant uses its own FTP client, and thus, can send files to a local FTP server. remotedir is the attribute that tells Ant the location of the remote directory on which we will be performing our actions. The action attribute tells Ant what to do on that directory. All our standard FTP commands, for example, get/put, are available via the action attribute.

```
<fileset dir="/tmp/ShelterSite" id="id">
```

Nested in the ftp element is the fileset tag. The dir attribute specifies the local root directory we wish to use. Combined with the previous ftp element's action and remotedir attributes, Ant will send this local directory to the remote directory.

You may have created this build file underneath the project directory and checked it into CVS. This is not a bad thing because you now have a history of a file that is a critical piece of the project. However, it is a bad thing if it gets FTPed into the production web server, especially if you have FTP server passwords! We should also prevent Eclipse from uploading its own .project file to the web server.

```
<exclude name="**/build.xml*/" />
<exclude name="**/*.project" />
```

To exclude the build and .project files from the upload, we use exclude elements for these two files nested within fileset. There is a corresponding include element to specify the inclusion of files. For both elements we name our file using the name attribute. Ant includes a powerful pattern-matching engine for use in include and exclude. In our example, the first exclude tells Ant to exclude anything named build.xml from the upload process. The second tells Ant to exclude anything ending with .project from the upload process. Be aware that the order of include and exclude tags is important in a fileset element, with the lower include/exclude taking precedence over previous ones in case of conflict. For example, if you tell Ant to include a directory, you can name specific files to exclude within that directory by placing the exclude tags after the directory include tag.

```
        </fileset>
      </ftp>
    </target>
```

Finally, we close out the `fileset`, `ftp`, and `target` elements in this block.

```
    <target name="cleanUp">
      <delete dir="/tmp/ShelterSite"></delete>
    </target>
  </project>
```

At the end of the file, we clean up our temporary directory. We do this with our fourth target. The only task in here is a `delete` task. It identifies which local directory we want to delete with a `dir` attribute. Lastly, we close our `project` element. Our build file is complete. It's time to run our file.

Running an Ant Script

To run an Ant Script, select the `build.xml` file in the Navigator view. Select the Run | External Tools | Run As | Ant Build menu option. Eclipse will automatically trigger the build file. The results of our execution will be output in the Console view.

```
Buildfile: /Library/WebServer/Documents/ShelterSite/build.xml
startPublish:
getFilesFromCVS:
      [cvs] cvs checkout: Updating ShelterSite
      [cvs] U ShelterSite/.project
      [cvs] U ShelterSite/CatAction.php
      [cvs] U ShelterSite/ViewCats.php
      [cvs] cvs checkout: Updating ShelterSite/classes
      [cvs] U ShelterSite/classes/clsCat.php
      [cvs] U ShelterSite/classes/clsCatView.php
      [cvs] U ShelterSite/classes/clsDatabase.php
      [cvs] U ShelterSite/classes/clsPet.php
      [cvs] cvs checkout: Updating ShelterSite/styles
      [cvs] U ShelterSite/styles/shelter.css
startFTP:
      [ftp] sending files
      [ftp] 7 files sent
cleanUp:
    [delete] Deleting directory /tmp/ShelterSite
BUILD SUCCESSFUL
Total time: 8 seconds
```

If there are any errors during the execution, they will also output here to help you troubleshoot.

Avoid Putting FTP Passwords in Build Files

You may want to avoid putting passwords in build files, since they are simple text files. To do this, reference them with a dollar sign and bracket: `${ftpPassword}`. When you execute the file, pass in an argument. To pass Ant arguments in Eclipse, go to the Run | External Tools | External Tools... menu option. Ant files have configuration profiles much like debugging configurations. This window will pull up the configuration for a particular Ant file. Highlight the build file you wish to work with and in the Main tab's Arguments area, type in -DftpPassword="YourSecretPassword" where `ftpPassword` is the name of the variable you specified in the build file and the enclosing quotes hold your password. Note the dash at the beginning of the argument and that there is no space after the D flag and the variable name.

Ant Tools

While Ant does not have its own perspective in Eclipse, it does have its own view and leverages the existing Outline view. Both are very helpful in developing Ant files for your projects.

The Ant view allows you to manage Ant build files in your workspace. It offers an overview of the build file and all its targets. You can add other build files to this view, execute them, and delete them via the icons in the toolbar.

When you are editing an Ant build file, the Outline view will give you structural information about your file. Organized by targets, the view gives you information on tasks and important parameters in the build file.

Summary

In the final step of our development, Eclipse also helps by providing tools to help with the deployment of our site. Using the FTP and WebDAV export plug-ins of the JDT, and the Klomp SFTP plug-in, we can directly push a site to a web server. In more controlled environments, we can automate this process by creating Ant build files. While writing Ant build files may involve more work initially, we save time in the long run because Ant can automate the tedious movement of deploying files, automatically grab the source files for us in CVS, and reduce human error in the process. Eclipse also helps us in creating Ant files with a built-in Ant editor and tools to execute and manage Ant build files. Initially built for Java, the use of Ant is just another example of the flexibility of Eclipse for all development, including for PHP-driven sites.

Plug-ins and Plug-in Sites

A critical element of the success and enthusiasm of the Eclipse ecosystem is the supporting community. A large section of this community focuses around the many plug-ins available. Here are some important plug-in sites and other useful plug-ins that you may find helpful as a web developer.

Community Sites

There is a healthy abundance of sites that focus on Eclipse in general or Eclipse for Java development, and a smaller number devoted to the plug-in community.

Eclipse.org

http://www.eclipse.org/community/index.php

Eclipse.org has a well-rounded community resources section. Among the sections housed here are Eclipse books, training, a list of plug-in repositories, a basic list of open source plug-ins, and a list of commercial plug-ins.

Eclipse Plugin Central

http://www.eclipseplugincentral.com/

Eclipse Plugin Central might be the most active Eclipse community site today. In addition to an expansive plug-in directory, this site hosts a very active Eclipse-oriented forum community, timely news headlines, and a classified ads system.

Eclipse-Plugins.info

http://www.eclipse-plugins.info/eclipse/

Eclipse-Plugins.info is a very comprehensive repository for both commercial and open source plug-ins. The site also allows visitors to leave comments and feedbacks about plug-ins. Between Eclipse Plugin Central and Eclipse-Plugins.info, every released plug-in is probably cataloged.

Eclipse-Workbench.com

http://www.eclipse-workbench.com/jsp/index.jsp

While the plug-in directory at Eclipse-Workbench.com may not be as comprehensive as the previous sites, it is a sizeable collection. Further, Eclipse-Workbench.com hosts a library of FAQs and articles related to Eclipse and the plug-in architecture.

Notable Language Plug-ins

For multi-lingual web developers, there is an Eclipse plug-in for almost every web development language. You will never have to leave Eclipse to build a web application. This is a listing of plug-ins for the more popular languages. All of these plug-ins are either free or open source.

Language	Plugin
C/C++	Eclipse C/C++ Development Tools `http://www.eclipse.org/cdt/`
C#	Improve C# Plugin `http://www.improve-technologies.com/alpha/esharp/`
ColdFusion	CFEclipse `http://cfeclipse.tigris.org/`
J2EE	Lomboz `http://www.objectlearn.com/index.jsp`

Javascript	JSEclipse
	`http://www.interaktonline.com/Products/Eclipse/JSEclipse/Overview/`
	JS-Sorcerer
	`http://www.dhitechnologies.com/`

Perl	EPIC `http://e-p-i-c.sourceforge.net/`
PHP (Besides PHPEclipse)	TruStudio `http://www.xored.com/trustudio`
Python	PyDev `http://pydev.sourceforge.net/`
Ruby	Ruby Development Tools `http://rubyeclipse.sourceforge.net/`

B

The Eclipse Update Manager

The **Eclipse Update Manager** is a mechanism used by Eclipse to keep track of its own plug-ins. The Update Manager keeps track of plug-in versions, informs you if a newer version is available, and helps you install new plug-ins. In fact, PHPEclipse recommends that you install its plug-in via the Eclipse Update Manager.

In this appendix, we will take a look at how to use the Eclipse Update Manager to install plug-ins. We will use PHPEclipse as an example. We will also see how to use the Update Manager to update the plug-ins already installed as well as how to update Eclipse itself.

To access the Update Manager, go to the Help | Software Updates | Find and Install... menu option.

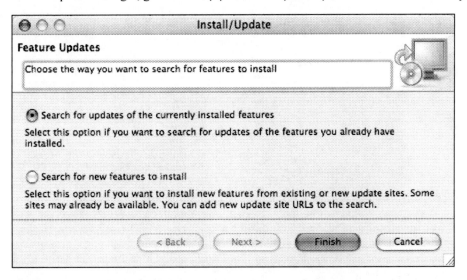

You will be given a choice to either update the currently installed plug-ins or search for new plug-ins to install.

Installing New Plug-Ins

The Eclipse Update Manager works by keeping track of the home update site of each plug-in. Eclipse aggregates this information in a file named platform.xml in the /configuration/ org.eclipse.update directory. To install a new plug-in, we need to tell the Update Manager where to grab it. We will walk through this process using the installation of PHPEclipse as an example.

Launch the Eclipse Update Manager. Select Search for new features to install and then click on the Next button. We will be presented with a list of software site bookmarks.

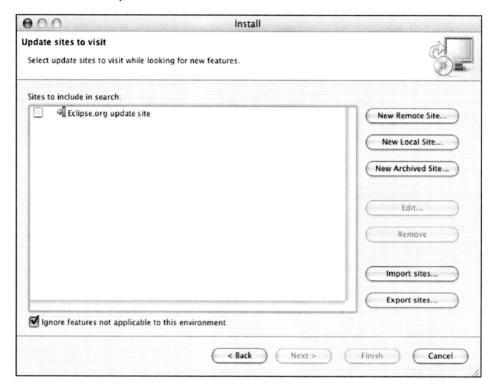

By default, Eclipse.org update site is pre-loaded so that Eclipse can update itself. This is a graphical, bookmark representation of the information stored in the features directory. You can edit and manage all your update sites by returning to this screen. Each bookmark in this list will be checked in the future when Eclipse searches for updates. When we add a bookmark for PHPEclipse, we are not only installing the plug-in, we are also telling Eclipse to automatically check for updates in the future.

If you stored a plug-in locally, you could also add a local file path as a site. You might want to do this if you were developing your own plug-in.

Installing PHPEclipse

Right now, we are going to add the official PHPEclipse update site as a repository. Click on the New Remote Site button. A small dialog box will appear allowing you to name the bookmark and enter a URL for the site.

Give the bookmark a descriptive name. The URL for the PHPEclipse site is http://pipestonegroup.com/eclipse/updates. Enter this information into the dialog box and click the OK button to add the bookmark.

Eclipse will query the site for available plug-ins.

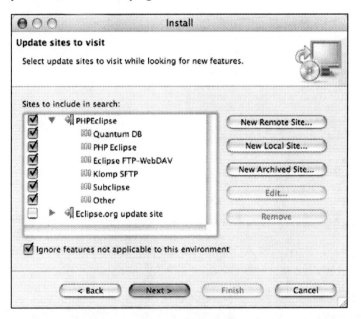

Select the plug-ins in the PHPEclipse package that you want to install. In this book, we use all of the plug-ins available, but at the minimum, you will need the QuantumDB plug-in and PHPEclipse plug-in. Click on the Next button to continue.

Eclipse will query the update site for the latest version available of the software package, and display all of the available components for installation.

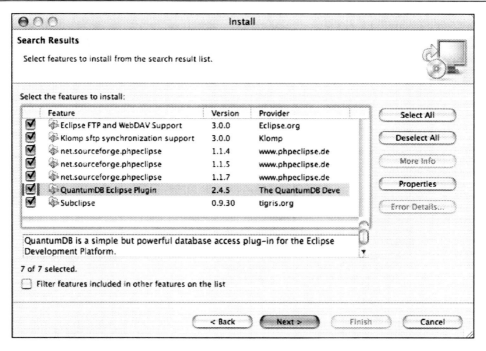

Click on the checkboxes for the items you wish to install. Click on the Next button to continue.

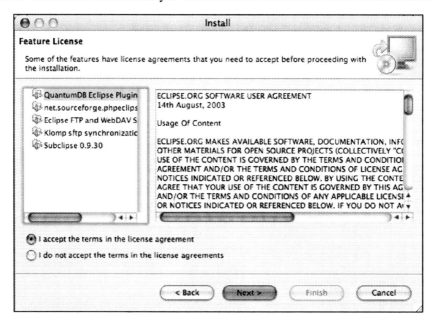

Read this license agreement. If you agree to the terms, make sure the first radio button is selected and then click on the Next button.

Finally, you will confirm your update and verify the location to install the files.

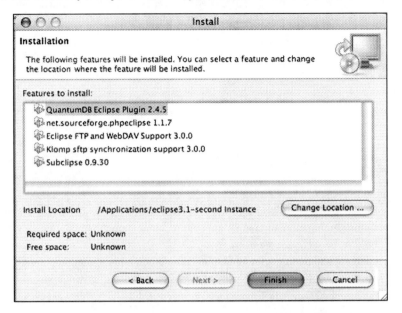

Verify your desired installation and its location. Click on the Finish button. PHPEclipse will be installed on your workstation.

You may receive warnings about some downloads being unsigned and untrustworthy. This is a security feature of Eclipse, which helps prevent the installation of potentially harmful software. Eclipse will look for a digital signature at the download site. If it doesn't find one, it will ask you if you still want to install the plug-in. Eclipse will give you information about the download URL and who it thinks is the manufacturer. You can read this information and if you still feel comfortable with downloading the plug-in, continue with the process. Currently, PHPEclipse and its packages do not have a signature, but as long as you download it from the pipestonegroup.com site, you can trust the download.

When the download is completed, you will need to quit and restart Eclipse in order to load the new plug-in.

Updating Current Software

The process of updating installed plug-ins is similar to installing new plug-ins. The update process also uses many of the screens seen in the installation process. However, since Eclipse already knows the update location, we do not have to enter any sites. Instead, we just tell Eclipse to query the sites and compare the installed version to the latest version. To start updating, go back to the Eclipse Update Manager. This time, select Search for updates of the currently installed features on the main selection screen. Eclipse will automatically start comparing the installed software with the creators' software. If it finds an available update, it will appear in an available updates list.

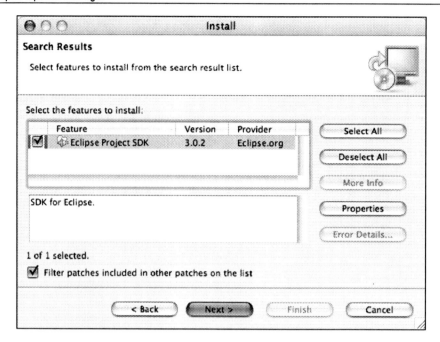

On this screen you will be able to review the plug-ins that need updates. You will also see a detailed description of each plug-in. Select the checkbox next to each plug-in you wish to update and click on the Next button.

From this point on, the process is exactly the same as installing plug-ins. Eclipse will present the software licenses for each plug-in, allow you to verify the installation location, and then start the download. Quit and restart Eclipse to take advantage of the new versions.

If you have not updated in a while, you may want to repeat this update process immediately after restarting Eclipse. You may not have the most up-to-date version of certain plug-ins. Some plug-ins have a dependency on a certain prior version of the same plug-in, or may have a dependency on another plug-in's version. Only when nothing appears on the list of available plug-ins is your Eclipse installation completely current.

Index

Error Log view, Eclipse, 113
error reporting, HTML Tidy, 92
exporting a project, FTP, 186
Expressions view, Eclipse debugger, 127

F

fatal error icon, Eclipse Editor, 68
features directory, Eclipse, 29
Files tab, phpDocumentor, 96
FileZilla Server Interface, 184
Filter option, Quantum Table view, 149, 150
folder mapping, 62
Folding tab, Editor preferences, 70
FTP export, 186
FTP server setup
　　Linux, 186
　　Macintosh, 185
　　Windows, 183

G

global tag, phpDocumentor, 95

H

historical preservation, version control, 157
Hover tab, Editor preferences, 70
How to handle dependent entities, Quantum
　　DB, 153
HTML code cleanup, 91
HTML Editor, WTP, 89
HTML Tidy, 91

I

IDE. See Integrated Development
　　Environment
implicit_flush directive, php.ini, 104
import a project, 177
Import/Export Bookmarks option, Database
　　Bookmarks view, 147
Improve C# language plug-in, 200
include files, 121
Insert Variable... button, code templates, 65
Install/Update screen, Eclipse Update
　　Manager, 201
installation
　　Ant, 192

Apache, 17
CVS server, 159
DBG, 100
Eclipse, 26
Eclipse debugger, 100
Eclipse plug-ins, 202
Java, 25
MySQL JDBC driver, 140
PHPEclipse, 29
XAMPP, 17
XDebug debugger, 130
Integrated Development Environment
　　advantages, 6
　　development project lifecycle, 7
　　disadvantages, 6
　　features, 5
Integration build, Eclipse, 27
internal tag, phpDocumentor, 95
interpreter, 105
Interpreter tab, Eclipse debugger, 111

J

JAR drivers, 143
Java Database Connectivity, 138
Java installation
　　Linux, 26
　　Mac OS X, 25
　　testing, 26
　　Windows, 25
JDBC, 138
JDBC Driver view, Quantum DB, 142
JDBC driver, adding, 142
JDBC-ODBC Bridge, 139
JDT, 9
JSEclipse language plug-in, 200
JS-Sorceror language plug-in, 200

K

keys, relational database, 138
Klomp plug-in, 187

L

Language pack, Eclipse, 28
language plug-ins, 200
link tag, phpDocumentor, 95
Link to folder in the file system checkbox, 62
Lomboz language plug-in, 200

Thank you for buying
PHPEclipse: A User Guide

Packt Open Source Project Royalties

When we sell a book written on an Open Source project, we pay a royalty directly to that project. Therefore by purchasing *PHPEclipse: A User Guide*, Packt will have given some of the money received to the PHPEclipse project.

In the long term, we see ourselves and you—customers and readers of our books—as part of the Open Source ecosystem, providing sustainable revenue for the projects we publish on. Our aim at Packt is to establish publishing royalties as an essential part of the service and support a business model that sustains Open Source.

If you're working with an Open Source project that you would like us to publish on, and subsequently pay royalties to, please get in touch with us.

Writing for Packt

We welcome all inquiries from people who are interested in authoring. Book proposals should be sent to authors@packtpub.com. If your book idea is still at an early stage and you would like to discuss it first before writing a formal book proposal, contact us; one of our commissioning editors will get in touch with you.

We're not just looking for published authors; if you have strong technical skills but no writing experience, our experienced editors can help you develop a writing career, or simply get some additional reward for your expertise.

About Packt Publishing

Packt, pronounced 'packed', published its first book "*Mastering phpMyAdmin for Effective MySQL Management*" in April 2004 and subsequently continued to specialize in publishing highly focused books on specific technologies and solutions.

Our books and publications share the experiences of your fellow IT professionals in adapting and customizing today's systems, applications, and frameworks. Our solution-based books give you the knowledge and power to customize the software and technologies you're using to get the job done. Packt books are more specific and less general than the IT books you have seen in the past. Our unique business model allows us to bring you more focused information, giving you more of what you need to know, and less of what you don't.

Packt is a modern, yet unique publishing company, which focuses on producing quality, cutting-edge books for communities of developers, administrators, and newbies alike. For more information, please visit our website: www.PacktPub.com.

Printed in the United States
70925LV00004B/158